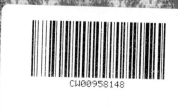

PETE BURNS
Freak Unique

PETE BURNS

Freak Unique

MY AUTOBIOGRAPHY

WITH IAN CRANNA

JB
JOHN BLAKE

Published by John Blake Publishing Ltd,
3 Bramber Court, 2 Bramber Road,
London W14 9PB, England

www.blake.co.uk

First published in hardback in 2006

ISBN 1 84454 298 X

British Library Cataloguing-in-Publication Data:

A catalogue record for this book is available from the British Library.

Design by www.envydesign.co.uk

Printed in Great Britain by Creative Print & Design, Ebbw Vale, Wales

1 3 5 7 9 10 8 6 4 2

Papers used by John Blake Publishing are natural, recyclable
products made from wood grown in sustainable forests.
The manufacturing processes conform to the environmental
regulations of the country of origin.

Photographs p2, p13 © Rex Features; p3 © Jim Halley; p8, p12, p15 left
© Empics; p9 © James and James, retouching by Gozra; p11, p14
© Michael Simpson; p15 right © Getty and p16 © Michele Martinoli
with digital retouching by Gozra

Every attempt has been made to contact the relevant copyright-
holders, but some were unobtainable. We would be grateful if the
appropriate people could contact us.

To Lynne Corlette, Eva Maria Bettinna Quittner
von Houdek, Giovanni Ferrando, Paulo, Marina Zacco,
Francis and Amy Burns

Above and beyond all to
Michael Anthony Simpson (My Key)

With special thanks to Maria Magdalena
Dietrich von Losch

acknowledgements

Thanks to Carl Amos, Ashley Price, Sue Breakell and Jackie Price, Rose Keefe at the official website www.deadoralive.net, Neil Simpson and for supplying pictures, Debbie Hoare, Dave Smalley, Judy Hyde, Dave Beaney, Marcus Stubbs and E Christopher Michaelson.

contents

a note from the publisher

The housemates were furious. The tabloids were raging. The police were called. Writing after the event it seems incredible that Pete Burns could have caused such a fuss by claiming he was wearing a coat made of your genuine gorilla. But everything Pete did in *Celebrity Big Brother* sparkled, rippled and caused a sensation. You loved him or you were repulsed by him – but you had an opinion. He's a natural star and it was a delight to get him to do his autobiography – he'd been threatening one for years and it was a thrill to work on it.

When it came to meeting him, he surprised all over again. Pete wasn't out to shock, to upset, to outrage, he wanted only to work hard, to present himself honestly and to reach as many people as possible. He was as outraged as anyone else about the gorilla incident, but his feeling stemmed from wondering how on earth anyone could have taken such obvious flippancy seriously. Better the police were out catching serious criminals, he pointed out, than trying to get to him in the house.

This was Pete all over. Direct, forthright and expecting everyone around him to be the same. The famous Liverpudlian candour is strong in him and as long as you were not superficial or deceitful, he was easy to get along with. His attitude to his career was just the same – keep moving on, don't waste time. And so work on the book began immediately.

Although he was beseiged with offers after *Big Brother*, Pete gave generously of his time and effort to make it happen in short order. In that he was helped by the start he'd made on it long before he even appeared on the show. This was the other great thing about him. Not only was he the star of *Celebrity Big Brother*, but he'd been around the music business for years. From punk through to new romantic and right up to the present day, he's been touring and recording and reinventing himself.

He knew what he wanted and he knew how he wanted it to look. For him, the book was just another artistic expression like a song or an album. So he made sure he had a say in everything and a positive piece of criticism. In return, everyone worked hard to make it happen. He had final choice of co-writer, he and his partner Michael came up with the cover concept and Pete himself chose the title. The book, he said on numerous occasions, wasn't going to be one of those self-satisfied pop music memoirs which are little more than a series of cosy anecdotes – this was going to be uncomfortable at times, but strong and honest. His approach was uncompromising but as much as it could be hard work, it was rewarding.

Pete gave great insight into his life, which hasn't been the comfortable existence enjoyed by so many rock stars, although once it seemed like it might turn out that way. Back in the 1980s, he'd seemed impossibly glamorous, an androgynous sex symbol who could be pinned up in anyone's bedroom. He was married, so the girls could safely lust after him, but his open attitude to sexuality made him attractive and interesting to anyone – gay, straight or whatever – who wanted something different from their pop music. Boy George was the one you could have taken home to have tea with your mum, Pete Burns was the one who always that bit more exciting. If there was any justice, he'd be as big a star today across the board, but marking out an unique path in that way requires incredible reserves of strength.

That's the other thing that's remarkable about meeting him. Despite his honesty, intelligence and wit, that air of self-assured superiority which characterises so many stars is curiously lacking in him. In many ways he seems fragile and almost vulnerable – there's a certain look in his eyes or perhaps the way he holds his head slightly to one side. It's as if he's put so much into creating himself and his work that he has nothing left to keep the world at bay.

That aspect of him came to the fore as work on the book drew to a close. It was creeping up for weeks and, although nobody around him could say a definite time when it happened, it tipped over into illness. To the desperate worry of everyone who knows him, Pete's enormous creativity has made him unbearably fragile.

For a while, it seemed as if the book might not go ahead at all. It was close to being finished, but was it right to bring it out now? In the end, taking soundings from his friends, colleagues and family, it was decided yes and everyone helped out as much as possible. In particular, his manager Aroon Maharajh provided great assistance, being determined that Pete's story should come out.

The distressing circumstances make this an unusual way to start a book. But Pete is nothing but honest and if his story is to be told, it should be whole and not the kind of celebrity puff-piece he hates so much. Everyone involved in this book wants him to bounce back and as much as anything else, this is a book for Pete Burns as much as it is about him.

L Randall
Editor

prologue

'I always knew exactly who and what I was... and it wasn't a kettle.'

Lights... and mirrors. There was no escaping them. The lights were blinding in the *Big Brother* house. I was there until the bitter end, and it's a miracle my retinas are still intact. What with the boredom, the inane chatter, the backbiting, the bitching and the mindless tasks, I'm still not sure how on earth I managed to get through it all.

I had imagined what it would be like before I went in – the cameras, the deprivation, the weird mix of 'celebrities' (the quiet ones, the mouthy ones, the almost-famous, the desperate, the self-obsessed and the utterly insane) and what we would do all day. I also wondered how I'd cope without my friends, my lover... there were many good reasons not to do such a stupid programme. Who was it who said, 'I don't do reality'? Oh, yeah. Me.

But there were lots of reasons why I should. If you were offered silly money to parade around in your kecks all day, and drink a plentiful supply of alcohol, wouldn't you jump at it? Even if you had to share a bedroom with 11 strangers? I knew it would be bizarre, and hoped I might get something out of it, but nothing could have prepared me for what we went through over those weeks in that shit-hole. Or what happened afterwards.

If I thought I was getting back to reality when I stepped out of the house, I had another think coming. That was just the start of the insanity. Something had changed and it took me a while to realise it. I usually just get on with my life, though a lot of people seem to find that hard to believe. They don't think Pete Burns goes to the shops. Well, I've got to eat, honey, and I'm not one of those divas who has an entourage to do everything for them. I wipe my own arse.

Before *Big Brother*, I didn't get that much attention paid to me in the street. Oh, sure, sometimes people shout things out; I got the odd 'Faggot!' Mostly I was able just to go anywhere on my own without any hassle, which was great as I love walking, anywhere and everywhere.

But when I got out of the house, Michael and I couldn't go anywhere without people stopping us. And you know what? It was all positive. I'd been allowed my voice on television and people really responded to that. It didn't matter who – from binmen to office workers, they all stopped me and they said I was brutally honest or they told me their life stories. I reflected what people thought. I was amazed, but the downside was it meant even a trip to the local shops would take forever. After a while, it became impossible to go out and do ordinary things.

And then there were the offers after the show. The media had seen what I could do and suddenly they all wanted me on their shows and in the newspapers. And this is after years of certain people in the business ignoring me when it suited them. But I've never wanted vengeance – I just want the truth. And I've heard every story that's perpetrated about me and it's nauseating that I have no voice. But guess what?

I'm back.

Now those same people are seeing me again and they're so nice to me, and I am nice back, but I can still remember what happened. So don't look me in the eye and tell me I'm so fabulous now, because I was just as fabulous then.

The business hasn't become any smarter. The record company re-released 'Spin Me' yet again. I mean, what is it with that song and the people who make those decisions? Even Judy Garland didn't constantly have to reissue 'Over the Rainbow' and it drove her half-mad. I'm very diplomatic. How very, very kind, but oh, enough already. I went back in the studio and started working on some new tracks, something very different. I was working all day and all night and I should have realised I was taking on too much.

Is this just another star moaning about their lot? Before you judge, remember that I'd spent 18 months in Italy undergoing reconstructive surgery to resolve those horrendous problems I'd had which started in my face and migrated to just about every part of my body. And, while people ogled and laughed behind their hands at the mess I became, I was on the verge of major organ failure. It wasn't a laughing matter.

In 18 months, I did nothing more than try to get well and try to keep going through endless painful procedures. I still don't sleep well and I'm often in a lot of discomfort. I am constantly having to be monitored. I don't know if I was ready for the spotlight to be on me this relentlessly and, within weeks of leaving *Big Brother*, I was suffering from sleep deprivation and exhaustion. And yet I knew what to expect when I entered the *Big Brother* house. I've come through worse, so don't cry any tears for me just yet.

In a way, I had been prepared for years. *Big Brother* wasn't real life, it was only a TV show, an extension of what we had all been doing in our normal lives anyway. We were all used to being on show, in one form or another, so it was really no hardship to be *on* a show, however weird the circumstances. And I've been through enough in my life to feel that, whatever they threw at me, whoever I met in there, I'd be able to cope, and come out smiling. And I did.

I do draw the line somewhere, though. I wouldn't do anything, for example, without looking my best. That is my rule, and it is one I have lived by since the year dot. My make-up regime, my clothes, my hair… they're an integral part of me, and no matter what *Big Brother* cooked up to humiliate, deprive and punish us with, I was determined to hold on to a few of the things that have become essential to who I am. My outer and inner identity.

So I had to be grateful for those lights and mirrors. As I stared hard enough into the depths of one of those reflective surfaces, I could see the ghost of a camera lens unblinking in the twilight world beyond. I appreciated this time, this quiet time, in which I could construct the visual persona that would be presented to the world. And as the foundation, the lip gloss and the mascara went on, so the camera remained immobile, but watchful, dumbly recording every movement, every lick of paint.

I was that camera once, staring in boyish wonder at the transformation being performed in front of me. And of all the images that shimmer and dance uncertainly in the memory, I keep returning to one – my mother, doing exactly as I do now.

1
bright sparks

'I used to put on Mum's stiletto boots and mime in the mirror to Nancy Sinatra. I wanted to be her, really. And here I am.'

My mother… her make-up… and it's four o'clock in the morning. Those are the first memories I have from when I was really young. At that time, she had decided to stop sleeping with my dad. She thought that the world, or your man, should only see 'your beauty', and beauty was artifice, and it took ages to put on, so don't let anyone see it dissolve! So she no longer shared a bedroom with him. I slept with her from then on, but I always remember the darkness of being woken and carried downstairs and taken into the living room.

We had a three-bedroom house in Port Sunlight in Cheshire – it was really quite a nice house. The living room had two glass panels in the door, and I remember a piece of fabric being pinned over the door windows and the inner curtains being drawn, and a heavy chair being put up against it at an angle to block out any intruders. And I remember being put on the sofa, still asleep, with one of her fur coats over me. How camp is that? Then being given a bacon sandwich or something when I woke up.

I remember seeing her remove lampshades from table lamps, change bulbs, put a white or pink cloth on the dining-room table, position the lamps, position a magnifying mirror in the middle of this, and another large wall mirror 3 feet in front of all this. Then she'd bring out a bone china saucer, and several bags or shoe boxes of make-up, tweezers and those steel contraptions I now know to be eyelash curlers. It was just magical – I thought I was watching a great artist at work.

I distinctly remember her taking a lighter or a match, holding it under the china saucer until it was blackened, then putting Vaseline on her finger, wiping it on the black soot, before blending the tiniest bit into her eye socket. She said that, if you do one creative thing to start the day, it made for a better day.

Maybe these philosophies are not considered unusual today and, to me, they never were. But to the outside world at that time in the early 1960s in England, they were little short of insanity. I came to realise this as I started to try to make my way in the 'real' world. It didn't reflect badly on her in my eyes; I just thought the real world was full of people who were retarded, and really missing out on something. They spent all their time criticising or thinking about other people's lives, when they were really missing out on time for and with themselves, to dream of being something better than maybe they were. Even if the rest of the day turns out to be a total nightmare, at least you have had that dream time – you, the mirror and make-up.

So I remember sitting there, watching her paint a picture. That, and the radio being on a lot – Radio Caroline. She always liked the radio on when she was doing her face. Then daylight would filter through gradually, the chair would be removed, her clothes would be on and then it was like the whole building awoke.

My dad worked in Lever Brothers' factory. By the time I became aware of what he did for a living, he was the managing director of Lever Brothers. He started at the bottom and worked his way up, but, at the time of my first memories, he was blue collar. The house was provided by the firm. It had no heating, and we had no phone – it was a nice house but it was the coldest place in the world.

My dad would have left by 8.30 in the morning but he used to come home every lunchtime and he'd come home every evening. At weekends, he'd lie in and maybe take me to Liverpool, which seemed like a very glamorous destination – a city! On Sundays, he'd watch TV and read the papers. But I don't think that shows any kind of neglect on my dad's part. I was just closer to my mother – and he knew it. He didn't try to impose any discipline in terms of my schooling, or worry about me.

Other people who've heard this think, 'Oh, he must have been indifferent,' but he really wasn't.

Sometimes, people are a quiet strength, you know. He loved my mum passionately and she wasn't an easy ride. My dad was invisible because my mum was such a firework display. She made me seem passive. But she was the best firework display in the world, even when it was really a load of old bangers. My mum could be a sparkler, and then she'd become a Catherine wheel, and sometimes she was just a banger... and then she went back to being a sparkler.

And my dad was so great with it. He loved her so much. He never wandered, he never condemned her, but he couldn't help her with the alcoholism. He didn't even really see it. She only got drunk in the afternoon. She was unconscious by the time he got home at night and my dad would go, 'Oh, Peter, don't be so dramatic – your mother's tired.'

He had his own way of dealing with it and the last occasion he had to, it was a Christmas when my mum was sitting in a chair and she kicked my dad in the back and he fell into the fire. I said, 'She's drunk!' and he was going, 'She's not drunk!' as he beat the flames out of his sweater.

He had to let her go on her own journey, but he was there... sometimes, it's not so much what you do as the fact that you're there, because she'd have died alone. He kept the home fires burning financially, the roof over our head, because the house was provided by the firm – so he was there.

And when she decided she was leaving him to have a relationship with me, because I was the late-born, the gifted one, he was still there. And he was a good ten years younger than her. He was the one who first told me the phrase that truth is stranger than fiction, because I'd ask about Mum and he would say, 'The truth is an awful lot stranger than fiction, son.' I only ever got fragments from her, such as 'and now all of my family are dead...' and stuff like that – but, when I was so young, it sounded like a movie to me.

I was brought up to believe that my mother, Eva, was Austrian. Only two or three years ago, I found her passport and discovered that she was born in Heidelberg in Germany, and she had a sister called Erna. Her father, Hugo Quittner, either owned or was a director of Babelsberg Studios in Berlin. There were a lot of family photos with the film star and singer Marlene Dietrich, particularly of my mother's father with her. I know he either directed or produced films that she'd starred in, and that she did 12 silent movies. My mother had attended silent-film school, and her family was very rich. My mum's mother was German, and her father was Jewish, so he went into hiding and my mother continued to live in one of the apartments they owned – of which there were several – so I can only gather it was Berlin or Vienna.

One day, she went to see her father, but her chauffeur had betrayed him to the Nazis – he was gone. She had cabbages thrown at her in the street. Her mother, Maria Quittner, was beaten up; the film studios were burned.

Then she seems to have spent some time on the run. She married a Baron Friedel von Hudec, so she got a title. He had the lifestyle, and she had a chinchilla dressing gown, so, despite it still being wartime, she was protected.

Then there's a hole in the story. A lot of American soldiers came to the apartment; she had to go to bed. She got up one night and found her husband having sex with several of the American soldiers for favours. He had no money, although he had a title, and he was very beautiful, and she had no idea he was servicing the soldiers. There was violence. She fled. She got a job in an exclusive clothing shop, but nobody had any money except for prostitutes, so she was selling clothes to prostitutes. She sold more than anybody.

Sometime during this period, her mother developed brain cancer. They were still on the run; they changed identities; and then she met somebody called Luigi, an Italian Mafioso guy. She was courted royally, and was lavished with black diamonds, opals... the works. When her mother died, she had the best for her funeral, all these black horses with plumes. She's got a sort of marble mausoleum, apparently, but I don't know where it is. I would really love to go and see it, but I don't have a clue where to start.

Then there was a daughter, then a blitz. The daughter was killed in a bomb shelter. Her sister Erna fled to the mountains and my mother was homeless. Then there's another gap.

When my dad met her at a soldiers' tea dance in

Vienna, she was apparently working for the Russian secret police. She was called Stara Baba – 'old woman'. She had Russian papers so she was exempt from any bother wherever they were. There was an incident with the Russian secret police because she was staying with my father in her apartment. They kicked the door in, and all hell broke loose as she attacked the soldiers. Dad said he'd never seen violence like it in his life, the way my mother went at the soldiers.

Then she became pregnant with my brother Tony, and my dad was obviously patriotic and he wanted his son to be born under the English flag. This would be 1946 or 1947. By this time, my father had seen the concentration camps and everything. He never got to see where my mum really lived. They used to meet and enjoy each other's company in a special apartment, and they spoke in French with one another.

My dad's very witty and dry but he could never get rid of, in his words, her 'fucking brother and her sister' – they were always around. When they went to the station to go back to England, he thought, 'Shit, they're coming, too... she's going to bring her brother and her sister.' It turned out one was her wig-maker and one was her masseur. They were living in cellars at the time but she kept her wig-maker and her masseur. And he said she got on the train in a long badger-skin coat with badgers' heads. She never lost her aristocratic ways.

When she got to Anfield, Liverpool, she thought she was in the servants' quarters. She was surrounded by doors that wouldn't open for her. She'd never boiled a kettle in her life. She thought my dad's mother must have been the cleaner, and it didn't help that she spoke no English. When my mother would call for my dad downstairs, when my brother Tony was born, my dad's mother would go, 'Oh, these bloody continentals, they can't get enough of it!' But Mum didn't know what that meant – no English.

When she went round Liverpool at that time, she used to take a piece of chalk with her and chalk her way round. She couldn't ask the way back.

But the most amazing thing – my dad still tells me to this day he doesn't know how she got it or what she did with it – was that she brought with her an ingot of gold bullion in a loaf of bread. Where had she got it? He doesn't know. But it was in a hollowed-out loaf of bread. She'd quite innocently passed right through all the borders with it. He said it was real gold bullion. Where did it go? He doesn't know. But he also said she was trading on the black market – silk stockings, sardines – so she could have been decapitated abroad for what she was doing.

This is her story. I will never really know it all, because she destroyed most of her things when she had her nervous breakdown later. I've got photos of her with Dietrich, but there's a big rip down the middle. My dad just doesn't go there. I don't know if it's because I don't push him enough.

What happened next I'm not sure, but she had tried to

find out about her dad, and I remember this day – it was a Saturday morning – the windows of the living room were black, there were candles and this awful sound. Oh my God, the awful sound – *kaddish*, the Jewish mourner's prayer. She'd received a bundle of papers. Her father had been drowned in the transport to a concentration camp; he'd obviously drowned in his own piss. She'd received letters begging her to bring him a gun. They'd broken his legs and he was naked in the snow and he was in a school that was less than a hundred yards from where she lived. And she could have got him a gun and she would have got him a gun.

But, to add insult to injury, all these years later she found out her sister Erna had already got all of the war compensation and had bought herself a tidy little mansion in Salzburg and had known about it for years. She was living in this beautiful mansion in a place called Traumstrasse – Dream Street – in Salzburg, right next to the Mirabel Gardens, where they filmed *The Sound of Music*. Erna had got everything, while the family had lost art, sculptures, famous paintings, the lot.

So she completely broke down and, of course, the doctor was called in. And you can guess the rest – Librium... Valium... Purple hearts... 'Can't sleep with purple hearts? ... Er, a glass of sherry – that'll help you sleep... Oh, you're getting too thin – drink a bottle of Guinness a day...'

And, combined with the grieving and the rage, she degenerated into an alcoholic – I hate that word to

9

describe her, but she had a really bad drink problem for many years and that's what drove me away from home at 14. I never went back, because I couldn't save her any more. To this day, I can't deal with alcoholism around me.

My dad worked all the time, and he sort of went into denial about it, but she'd usually be unconscious when he got home. I was the one who actually had to deal with it. She used to cut her wrists, but we had no phone for the ambulance. She'd hang herself. She used to turn the gas on and put her head in the oven after an overdose of Valium. I learned how to get into the house without moving the windows. The house had leaded windows, so the only way you could get in – because of the lead frame you couldn't push it without sparking – was to go round the lead with a fingernail and take a pane out and open the latch very gently. There were also pill overdoses.

I eventually got her taken into a psychiatric hospital by a social worker at Christmas. It was just a drying-out place. She came out two weeks later and she was feeling run down, so the doctor said, 'You need iron, and that's in Mackeson.' So the alcoholism started again... and then she had seizures when she stopped the Valium. She thought the telly was talking to her. And they'd come round and go, 'Take a Valium.' And hey presto – normal! So she was maintained on those things.

So how did I cope? I did what was necessary. I pulled the pills out of her throat when she was unconscious. I sat in the living room waiting to hear movement upstairs. The mornings were fabulous because the make-up was on. Then she'd go shopping. The food was done. Dad would go to work, then by three in the afternoon she'd go to bed – I was brought up on an afternoon-nap system. Sometimes, those afternoon naps became a bit more sinister. I was getting older and I wasn't going to go for an afternoon nap, but she was upstairs in the bedroom and I remember listening all the time. I knew every sound in the ceiling – where she was moving.

So then I got to watch a lot of black-and-white Hollywood movies – there used to be afternoon films on BBC2 then – and that's where I saw all the early Monroe films. I'd have the set on low and I'd listen, and sometimes I'd hear an unusual noise. On one occasion, I went upstairs and the door was barricaded, so I pushed it and, when I'd opened it sufficiently, I could see her lying on her side and she looked round. I went over to the bed and she'd nearly severed her hands. We had no phone, so I had to run to every neighbourhood house, banging on the door. I couldn't get into the factory to see my dad – I think he was away on business – so I just ran and ran.

I did manage to get help from somebody called Auntie Gladys – she was a neighbour and she wanted to come and see, but she lived at number 31 and we lived at number 6. I made the call, and the next thing I remember was the ambulance coming – they took one look at her and they actually drove up on to the lawn and broke the doorframe of the house to get in that quickly. And that wasn't the only time.

But, if you think it was bad for me, imagine how she felt to do that. A hundred times worse, because she wasn't doing it as a cry for help – she wanted to die. And she wanted to die by her own hand, and I think that's quite a powerful way to die; to make your own choice, no going back, not feeling sorry for yourself – 'Right, I'm going to do this.' If I had that button with a terminal illness, I'd want to be the one to press it. It's empowering.

And, when, as a child, you know no other way, you don't think anything is wrong. I never once felt like I needed Mum to look after me. I really felt I was there with the sole purpose of looking after her in some way. Just making her time better. And we didn't have psychiatry then.

I still think psychiatry is highly questionable; where do you draw the line on what is mental illness? The witchdoctors in primitive tribes who hear voices and channel things – if they were in 'civilised' countries, they'd be sectioned under the Mental Health Act. Hundreds of years ago, people who were healers – homeopaths – were burned at the stake. So where do you draw the line?

I've cried my tears, but I've dried my face now. I don't want anyone to say I had a terrible mother, because she was absolutely the best mother in the world. I wouldn't have had it any other way. I wouldn't have wanted a mundane mother who said... whatever it is that mundane mothers say. Not by any means. How awful!

And don't get me wrong – it wasn't a Judy

Garland/Liza Minnelli situation, where I'd gone off to see the wizard. She was artistic and, in order to be artistic and creative, you've got to *feel* things a bit more. Your reds are redder, your blues are bluer. And, somehow, you feel those things and you pull them right back down and dilute them so people can understand them. She was very much like that and I think that's something that's inherent in me.

2
inside out

'You are what you eat, and who wants to be lettuce?'

I was born on 5 August 1959. It would have been a lot more interesting had it been 5 August 1962, because that would have coincided with the death of Marilyn Monroe and given my birthday some kind of edgy glamour. I could have made endless witty quips about it in print. I was denied this privilege, though I can vaguely remember the news of Marilyn's passing being a topic of discussion on and around my birthday that year. Somebody important, famous, had died. I remember my father, in particular, passing comment – something like it was because she wore too much make-up, was too blonde, too stupid, too sexy... too everything, in fact. She got what was coming to her.

The same opinion came from a few of the neighbours who would occasionally visit my mother for morning coffee and to have a look at me, a miracle baby, born to a mother 47 years old, which in those days was as good as dead. I remember that, when most of these visits took place, I was nearly always on my potty, in the middle of the living-room table. The act of moving one's bowels was very important to my mum, and every turd I produced was snatched, in the potty, from underneath me, passed around for inspection, then rewarded with a round of applause from her and anyone else fortunate enough to have been present to witness such a wondrous event. This, I have to point out, left me with no deep emotional scars or phobias.

My older brother Tony had been born in 1948, so there's a huge gap between us. (My life seems to be full of age gaps – my father was ten years younger than my mother, my brother eleven years older than me, and my current partner Michael is almost ten years younger than me.) I never really got to know Tony. I think he was at grammar school, and he'd come home at four o'clock in the afternoon and then he was off with his friends. But, thanks to his age and interest in 1960s pop music, Tony gave me early exposure to music and fashion of that time. There wasn't a day of my early childhood that wasn't drenched with the sound of the 1960s, usually filtered through the wall of the living room via the forbidden zone of the sitting room, which contained the glittering pink record player, the record collection and Tony.

Tony, I realised some time later, was an aspiring pop star. It was the time of the Beatles and various other Merseybeat pop sensations. He was young, owned a guitar and spent hours singing along to his records into a huge mirror. He was also in a group called The Coachmen and Jenny on the folk circuit. There were times Paul Simon came and slept on our sitting-room floor, before they did 'Sound of Silence', when they were struggling on the folk circuit. When they were on the road in those days, they just looked for accommodation where they could get it. Mary Travers of Peter, Paul & Mary slept there, too, because they were just in folk clubs then – they weren't stars. Liverpool wasn't far away and nor was Birkenhead, where there were folk clubs.

But they were nobody to me then. I was about four years old, I suppose. I don't think they even had records out then. I think it was before 'Scarborough Fair', and it was long before 'Leaving on a Jet Plane' and 'Blowin' in the Wind' and those records. But I do remember waking up one morning and this woman emerging from the sitting room. It was Mary Travers, with this platinum-white Egyptian bob, what I know now is like a broken nose and a square jaw, and she was kind of tall and big. And that made such an impact. At that time, I'd never seen anything like it.

There's an album called *Late Again* and a picture of her in profile on the back – she just looks so strong. The nose – look at the cover for yourself. Was it broken, or was it just strong? I used to show it to my dad and he'd go, 'She looks like a boxer.' I remember seeing that album cover and it was like, 'Oh my God... she stayed at our house!' I'd never seen anything as beautiful as that.

I then developed an obsession with some of Tony's record sleeves, but not those of the Beatles. The actual records were of little interest, as I didn't dare try to operate such a highly complicated device as the record player, let alone touch the vinyl discs contained within and smother them with fingerprints. But the covers... I could look at them for hours. Even now, just thinking about some of those images makes me want to search out those record sleeves – they just did something in my brain.

Later, my brother would watch the pop shows on a black-and-white TV, and a show came on with these two American Indians and I'd never seen two such good-looking people. It was Sonny & Cher. It was a very brief appearance and I just thought, 'Oh God, those men!' I had no idea she was a woman. I'd heard the voices and I still had no reason to suspect otherwise. That's not to say she looked like a bloke, but compared to Twiggy and Lulu – plus the black hair and the slightly bad skin and the strength of the features – oh my God. And I thought Sonny was equally as attractive.

I was too young then to be aware of many things, gender being one of them. I just knew what I thought was fabulous, and it more often than not had thick black eyeliner, teased-up jet-black hair, a pale-lipped smear, stiletto boots and came from America. That was just the way it was – nothing visually arresting came to my young eye via men or England. America gave me the record sleeves of The Ronettes, The Shangri Las, The Chiffons, Sonny & Cher and countless others. But mainly it gave me Veronica Ronette, with Cher a close second. Sound and vision... back then, I didn't care how it sounded; I only cared about the vision. Even today, I have to be attracted by the visual before I will listen, and that doesn't only apply to music.

Then there were the visual images of The Ronettes – newsflashes of a tour with the Rolling Stones – and I remember footage of the way they moved in very constricted Chinese evening dresses – *cheongsams* – that were so tight they couldn't really move about. They were knee-length and there was no high split, but there was something about the three of them doing these routines in dresses that were too tight that was really delicate. I remember the sight of the lead singer – it was like too much make-up, too much black hair and a big flower in her hair – I think they upstaged the Rolling Stones.

And then, shortly after that, I can remember my dad taking me to the cinema in Liverpool. I guess I was too young to appreciate the film – I was more interested in waiting for the ice-cream break – but I loved the size of the screen. And my dad was trying to tell me this film [*Funny Girl*] was about someone called Fanny Brice but I was too young. But then – gasp – there was this flash of someone in a leopardskin coat and they went up to the mirror and went, 'Hiya, gorgeous...' and it was Barbra Streisand, with short hair.

I didn't go to the cinema again for a long time, but, when I did, it was a Western, *Shalako*, and, for the first time, I saw this being called Brigitte Bardot at her peak. I loved Westerns – though now I find them traumatic because I'm obsessed with Red Indians – and I saw this scene of Bardot in a riding jacket and a diamond choker and what looked like the filthiest hair in the world and the blackest eyes. She looked to me like a Persian cat – gender didn't enter into it. It was just beauty to me.

I think it was more than beauty – there were things I *wanted* to look at. I had an obsession with drawing faces of that structure when I was very young. I always drew. I'd slice the pictures horizontally and move things about. I was always entering drawing competitions. When I was eight, I entered a competition in the *Daily Express* where I had to draw a Mary Quant design. I had flair as an illustrator and I won a whole set of Mary Quant make-up – Cheeky Chops and Jelly Babies (which was a jelly blusher) and a Mary Quant paintbox for eyes with all the numbered colours and a diagram and upper and lower lashes.

When I was in the Big Brother house, we were given this painting task – I hadn't painted since I was 14. Nine minutes to do that. And then everyone said, 'My God... you can paint!' That's what I did as a child. I drew and painted.

My dad was just so great. I think other people's perception of my dad is that he was cold, because he didn't offer opinions; he just let you be. He was very intellectual. Unless he could see you doing – or being or thinking or saying – something purely objectionable, it was very much 'whatever'.

So I heard pop music a lot when I was young, wonderful things – like the Walker Brothers. I heard it but I wasn't allowed near the record player, so it was always there in the afternoons when Tony came home and up until 8.00pm. It was in the next room, so I'd listen at the door. It was Tony's private thing. He was busy miming in the mirror with his guitar. Who wants a four-year-old around when they're fifteen and covered in pimples? These were never bad relationships – it was about giving people their space.

I remember sometimes his friends would come and they had a Mini Moke car, like a little jeep, and they'd drive on to New Brighton beach. I was too young to go but I remember the sounds of the Beach Boys and the Moody Blues' 'Go Now' and Linda Ronstadt's 'Different Drum'... They didn't make an impression as in 'I want to do that', they were just lovely sounds. And more often than not, if I rooted through the Welsh dresser where the records were kept, the lovely sounds had really lovely images with glossy fronts – sound and vision.

I also remember a show Rod McKuen had on BBC2. It started with a song called 'Mr Kelly' about a sheepdog. I was obsessed with Rod McKuen... *crazed* for Rod McKuen!

Bobbie Gentry! What did she have going on? That was something else altogether, and I don't mean 'I'll Never Fall in Love Again' – I mean 'Ode to Billy Joe' and the photographs of Bobbie Gentry.

The first concert I went to see, my dad bought me tickets for Esther and Abi Ofarim. Esther Ofarim! Sending off to record clubs for cheap albums – four for £1. I never could pay, because I had no money, but we sent for them – I just wanted the covers so I could look at Esther Ofarim. The Mamas & The Papas – something there, something in Mama Cass Elliot's voice. She went solo and my dad bought me tickets to go but she died. And I cried.

Melanie Safka – 'Ruby Tuesday', the Buddah albums. I answered some questions in *Disc & Music Echo*, and what do you know? I won every album by Melanie... with all the posters! I had all the posters on the wall. And there was a documentary on BBC1 about Melanie and she was singing 'Momma Momma' in the studio with a guitar. We didn't have videos in those days. It was just brief filmed glimpses on a black-and-white TV.

Then my brother moved to Germany and there he was – sitting on stage at Melanie's feet! Melanie was kind of famous in Germany and she used to bring the audience on stage. He brought an album home called *Candles in the Rain* – it was different from the British version and there was a photo of her on the back with little American flag bows in her hair – and this song, 'Lay Down', with the Edwin Hawkins Singers. And there was *Affectionately Melanie* and all these others. Then there was 'Brand New Key' and it's so *not* that. The first album, *Born to Be*, had the lyrics: 'Once I bought a curious bottle...' and I remember 'Bo Bo's Party'. My God! I'll cover that. And the cover, that red triple image! I've never lost those memories.

I lived, I know now, a very solitary childhood. I had nothing to compare it with, so it seemed fine to me. I rarely left the house. I didn't need to; I had a secret world I shared with my mother. In those early years, I couldn't possibly have wished for a better friend. I think society has given us lots of ideas as to what a mother should be, and I am sure, as a mother, she wasn't that great in society's eyes. But, for me, she was definitely everything I needed. She gave me the power to dream, the power to remove myself from where I might not be having any fun, and go inside my head and be somewhere else. A secret place. It's difficult to explain, but it's a way of blocking out certain things. You are still fully aware they are there, and you are in them, but you put a kind of soft-focus filter over them and sharpen the things you want to, move things around a bit. It's still all real, but you've put yourself somewhere else for a while.

Both my mother and I spent a lot of time doing this trick, together and alone. She was where she wanted to be and I just liked to go 'somewhere else' – mainly my tepee (wigwam) or underneath the dining-room table, I have no idea why, but Sunday was reserved for taking up residence in the bedroom wardrobe. Just lying flat on the floor of it, underneath the hanging outfits and on top of the shoes or folded clothes! The door was always tight shut.

I know, in those areas of my early childhood, I was given what I really needed, but sometimes I think it was in me anyway, maybe from a past life. I know I was always almost painfully aware I felt like I was inside myself, looking out from the inside. The best way I can describe that sensation is when I had this *Dr Who* Dalek suit. It had a huge domed, hard plastic headpiece, which was edged with a floor-length plastic tent-like affair, printed with silver circles, and with two plastic stick-like rods that stuck out as sort of arm replacements, with the sole purpose of killing earthlings! The dome-shaped headpiece had slits going round its circumference and they were the only way you could see out. I felt perfectly at home inside this contraption, and would spend hours walking around with it on, totally unaware I was physically inside something others would have found unbearably claustrophobic.

I sometimes ventured outside into the village wearing this, and other children would attack it with sticks and branches, banging away at the headpiece which, thank God, was rock hard and enabled me just to keep walking, repeating over and over in a robotic voice, 'I am a Dalek... Exterminaaate... Exterminaaate!' I could see my attackers, but they couldn't see me. All of my life I have felt that way, like I can see them but *they* can't see *me*. I felt older, like maybe I had forgotten some things, and that, instead of learning, I was getting a refresher course almost to jog my memory, like before a test or exam.

School was almost non-existent. They couldn't get me into a school – it was something to do with christening me. My mother didn't want me to be a Catholic but, in order to get me christened, we had to sign up for a

Catholic school. But I didn't start at one. I started at Church Drive, Port Sunlight. I remember being taken along with my bag of dolls, which I collected avidly. Always dolls.

Way before Sindy and Tressy, there were other dolls, and there was Honey West from an American TV series. She was like Emma Peel, the high-kicking ladette with the model looks from the TV show *The Avengers*, but she had an ocelot on a lead. Female detective dolls were a particular favourite – Honey West, The Girl from U.N.C.L.E. – always dolls. I also had Chief Cherokee and Mike Hazard, a detective doll with a trench coat and a suitcase that exploded. Chief Cherokee had a tepee, a horse, a rubber headdress that you built – loads of practical accessories. I collected models of things like Henry VIII and his six wives, painted Airfix models... so I may have been a loner, but I wasn't alone.

I remember my mother taking me to one of the infant schools and leaving me there, freaking me out. Then, the next thing I remember is my mother in the playground with that tepee at break-time, and all the kids were round the tent and she was giving them sweets. Then I just don't really remember going back – inside the school, that is. I think my dad thought I went, because a lot of performance was staged early in the mornings before he left for work – breakfast, getting dressed in school things and brandishing the pencil case. Then, once he was out of the door, it was me and her.

Eventually, though, discussions centred around getting

me admitted to the Catholic school – St John's in New Ferry – but it took months to get everything approved. My mother had it all worked out – I was always getting sick, always really ill. I mean, I didn't *feel* sick – I was just tucked up in bed with a mound of comics. She didn't tell me I was sick, she just told my dad I couldn't get out of bed. She'd come in with a flannel and wet my face and say, 'Look, he's in a cold sweat!'

If you got a doctor's note, you didn't have to go to school, and we had Dr Whitfield, who was Mum's friend. I was always getting a thermometer shoved in my mouth or being put in the airing cupboard – 'Stay in there, stay in there!' – so I thought it was really exciting in the airing cupboard. But then, when I'd come out, there was someone with a thermometer and the next thing I was off for six weeks. The airing cupboard made you clammy, you see. Scarlet fever! No, I wasn't sick, but she would keep me away from school.

I participated in this willingly, because then we'd go for long walks, collect dried leaves, and then we'd make things out of the dried-up leaves with gold paint, and the little fire was on and it was cosy, and then it was tea time. And Dad would come home, and on would come a series called *The Roaring Twenties* following the adventures of a girl called Pinky Pinkham, and then *Honey West*, the first US TV series centred around a female detective. Then we'd go to bed, and she'd do her beauty ritual and she'd tell some ghost stories and stuff and then we'd sleep. And then the make-up started and the next day we'd go out shopping.

Comics, comics, comics – always comics. They were American comics called *Creepy* and *Eerie* and *Vampirella* – beautifully drawn things, with loads of adverts for things I couldn't order because they were in dollars and you had to write off to America. 'One day you'll have all of this...' Mum spoke to me in German. By the time I was born, her English was as perfect as her flawless face, but we still spoke in German. She spoke to my dad in French so I couldn't understand, and I was just somewhere in the middle. But I could understand the French – I knew by the way they moved. Even today, I can understand languages by the way people move – you've only got to watch the head.

All through my early childhood, I wasn't aware that flowers bloomed and died. My mum had a garden in the backyard, and it was just beautiful, especially when it snowed. I used to just stare out of the window at it – roses, carnations, huge yellow sunflowers and the pinkest tulips, and sometimes the flowers were gold or silver. Even pearls grew there. I was later to learn that the flowers were all plastic, and, if ever a string of pearls broke, she'd throw those on, too. And we had movement, too – we'd paint the shells of the tortoises. I'll always remember her drawing back the curtains one day and saying, 'Look – all the snow has gone. Now we have the best garden in the village.'

I thought that was fabulous! For this one small sacrifice of reality, we had flowers in the rain or snow, even gold ones, which no other garden could boast. And they were bigger, brighter, just more fabulous than anything anyone else had. They didn't die, we could add to them, bring them indoors, throw bottles of perfume on them and savour the smell, then put them back again. It was pure logic to her, and still is to me. Why should things of beauty die and decay? She found a way around that, and she made me believe in the fantasy and larger-than-lifeness of her garden.

This was also a philosophy she applied to many different areas of her – and my – life. During the 1960s, wigs were a fashion, and she held wig parties. She'd struck some sort of deal with a wig-maker who would deliver boxes of what looked like scalps to the house, and then me and her would put them on to wig heads, all over the front sitting room. Then the house would come alive with music and neighbours who came to 'try and buy' at her hiked-up prices. I don't think she ever kept a penny of the profits; she took her profit in wigs, which she and I adapted, sewed two into one, improved or wore, mainly before bed, or to go to post a letter. She didn't need to wear wigs – she had fabulous hair – she just thought they were a sort of hat, or a toy, and better than the real thing. There was no need to grow, tint or even give a shit about them. They were good to go. I think she was really ahead of her time.

These wonderful, idyllic times are very much a part of my childhood, but there was that darker side. Sometimes, Mum was just so sad. It was just natural to me at the time, part of the rhythm of life, so I wasn't traumatised or anything. I just knew something had changed, like time had stood still. The air seemed thick as mud, and she would cry. I would cry. I just wished I could make her happy, and thought that crying must mean she was sick, or had pains, and I would watch over her while she slept her sad days away, and resolve somehow to become a doctor and make all of her pain go away. That was my first ambition, to become a doctor, have a doctor's bag and everything it contained and cure her of the sad pains.

Another perk of this obvious career choice was that I would get to marry Dr Kildare, who was an actor called Richard Chamberlain in an American TV show we were both just gaga about. I didn't see any reason at all that there might be something impractical or unusual about my decision to marry him. Why not? We would become a team dedicated to the sole purpose of taking away Mum's sad pains. How could he resist me?

Later, it got more complicated to hide me from school authorities – and Dad – but we pulled it off for the most part. I was in a secondary-modern school called Newchester Road School and I did go once or twice – I mean, one day a week and then maybe one day a month and then it was just too dangerous. Slade was one band breaking through at the time, and kids were wearing Crombies and Doc Marten's.

It was just unbelievable. There was one period after the summer holidays when I went back to school. I'd experimented with a product called Hiltone Hair Lightener and washed over it with a Harmony Chestnut

Semi-Permanent, and it went absolutely vivid aubergine. I thought, 'Yes, result!' but it didn't suit my skin tone so I had to get some foundation. Well, in assembly you were all allotted your forms when you arrived back at school, like 5A, 5B, 5C. I was first off the list – 'Oh great, I can go and sit down.' So I went and sat down in the classroom – they were all like prefabs with half a glass wall. I was first but nobody else seemed to come in and the entire school of at least 600 people all filed past to look at me inside this room. And I thought, 'Where are they all going? I'm in here on my own.' The teachers used to announce, 'Boys... and Burns,' when they addressed the class. But it didn't touch me, I didn't feel bullied. It kind of prepared me really well.

People ask if David Bowie was an influence, and Ziggy Stardust. I wasn't that aware of him wearing a dress because he wasn't mainstream when he wore one. A long time before I saw Bowie I had shaved off my eyebrows and was dyeing my hair with shoe polish. There were no crazy hair colours available then, you know – I'd put green shoe polish though my hair and things like that. There was also a programme called *Lift Off with Ayesha* in the afternoon, on which there was this man with lots of blue eye-shadow, a quilted suit and boxing boots with this fabulous orange hair, and he put his arm around Mick Ronson and I thought, 'Yes! There are others out there. They walk amongst us...'

But then I wasn't *that* impressed, because I was already doing a similar thing visually. I'd got *The Rise and Fall of*

Ziggy Stardust and the Spiders from Mars, but only because I went to a record shop to buy an Alice Cooper album and they'd sold out. I loved the cover, but I didn't really play it.

I was briefly at school for a while and everyone had to play a record – a chart record – in some kind of assembly, and I remember this absolute bastard – a skinhead type – who'd brought in a Slade one. Then he put on 'Lady Stardust' and they all started to point at me and thought it was a matter of hilarity. So then I went home and listened to the album more closely and I thought 'Lady Stardust' sounded fab to me. But everyone at school was going, 'Haaa!'

I didn't have friends as a kid but I wasn't lonely. What did I need kids for? What could they teach me? To this day, I know so many people but, if you can't bring me some piece of knowledge, I'm not interested. I don't say, 'Sit down – tell me something,' but most things people make conversation about I know about already. I don't know where this knowledge comes from. Want to talk about doctors? I know. Want to talk about an actress from the 1950s? I know. Want to talk about records? I know. Madonna's 'Sorry'… to me, the vocal line sounds a bit like 'I Heard It Through the Grapevine', so why do I need to listen to that? I've heard the track already. 'Frozen' by Madonna to me sounds something like a Fleetwood Mac track. 'Forbidden Love' – what was that? So I've sort of heard it all before.

There was one great family who lived near us called the

Beatties – Rita and Frank Beattie and their five kids – Brian, Caroline, Joanne... but they all had bicycles and I didn't. They were very active kids, but I was more interested in the house. All the kids were in bunk beds, all in one room. I didn't really want that for myself, but it was different, you know? The kids were more sporty, but the mum, Rita, seemed to get me. When my mum was drinking a lot, she would take me in for the afternoon, and she'd keep an eye on her and things like that.

I got friendly with Brian, Caroline and Joanne, but people didn't really come to my house. I didn't want them to, and this was even pre-drinking – but people just didn't visit. We were 'the Nazis'. Mum was a kind of hot-house flower in a quiet country village, what with the accent and the war memories, which probably carried on a lot longer than I was aware of. But I wasn't an outcast. These are things I would clearly define – I was *not* an outcast. I've been on the outside looking in for so long, but I wasn't shut out. I was watching... waiting.

3

dangerous liaisons

'I don't consider myself mildly eccentric. I'm not a camp, throwaway queen… I've made myself what I want to be, not everybody's cup of tea. And people wanna have a look at me. I fully accept that. People have always wanted to have a look at me.'

I had no awareness of sex when I was growing up, but I was very aware that something was going on at school. I didn't know what it was, but certain pupils – the real bully ones who fought and bashed every other kid up – were very nice to me. They weren't repelled by me; in fact, the more macho the boy, the fewer derogatory comments I received from them.

I remember in one class, there was a kid wanking under the desk next to me, and he'd go, 'Do you wanna finish me off?'

I wish I'd said something like, 'Certainly not... Put it on the mantelpiece and I'll smoke it later,' but I just said, 'No.' I didn't know what he was doing, and it stank.

Another time, I was at home one day in the front room, playing records, and someone knocked at the front door. It was that boy and one of his friends and they wanted to come in. I let them in and we were playing some records and he went, 'Do you want to wank me off?'

'No thanks,' I said, because I wasn't quite reading it then.

And then there was a legendary man called Simon. I think he was in his thirties, but he was legendary in the village and the surrounding areas because he dyed his hair. He was kind of an older macho man, with dyed blond hair which would sometimes be streaked. And he had a good car and nice clothes, but I didn't know that then – I just knew of Simon.

I was no longer attending school by then, but I knew they went off on school holiday trips, and Simon, because he was older, went on one of these school holidays – I don't know in what capacity. And the big talk of the trip was that he had wrestled to the floor that boy who'd come on to me, pulled his pants down and kissed him. My first thought was that he'd won a sort of victory over the boy. Then I became aware that Simon worked near by, and we'd see his car go past the house and we'd go, 'There goes Simon.' By that time, I think, there'd been whispers about him and he'd cruised past me in his car a few times and I'd seen him look.

34

Then I started to hear there were these clubs in Liverpool. I was a long way from Liverpool then, but there's a place called The Wiend, which was a very odd mixture of a shopping area and park. It was about 20 minutes from my house, which involved a nice walk uphill and under a bridge in my 5-inch platforms. There was a log that I used to sit on, and what do you know? Simon had to drive past to go home!

I just remember sitting there and thinking, 'He's going to notice me.' It wasn't a sexual thing – he just seemed so sophisticated. He had this car that was always blaring great music, like Suzi Quatro's 'Can the Can'. I was wild about Suzi Quatro – she was on *Top of the Pops* in a leather catsuit with that striking voice and the Red Indian-looking boyfriend, flicking that hair about... For a brief moment in time, I actually thought I might grow up to *be* Suzi Quatro – much more preferable to David Bowie! And I sat there for days at the same time.

Then I realised – he was on specific shift patterns – two o'clock in the afternoon, he clocks in four days a week, then he clocks off. So then I thought, 'Hold on, shifts have changed – now he's on the seven 'til ten.' So I would conveniently be waiting on the log!

Then he got a really flashy car, and eventually he made contact. He stopped right by me and asked, 'Do you want a lift?' And I was like, 'No.'

And the more snotty I got, the more interested he seemed. He'd park the car and he'd walk to the shops. He'd come back with a bottle and go, 'Hi! What are you doing here? Do you like this?' and I'd go, 'No,' or 'Bye, gotta go.'

But then it wasn't long before he said, 'Listen, some friends and I are going to go to this club in Liverpool, and we think that you would really like it. Do you want to come?'

'Yeah,' I said, and I thought, 'Shit, he thinks I'm a lot older than I am.'

So, on the Tuesday, I started to get ready, and, when Saturday came around, he picked me up in the car and he drove to Liverpool. There were two other people with us and I was taken into this gay club called The Bear's Paw. It was like a disco cave with a mirror ball. I think the first record I heard in there was 'Kung Fu Fighting'.

The clientele were an interesting bunch – there were the really camp ones who looked like Gilbert from *Not on Your Nelly* with big fur coats; hairdressers with highlights and glasses; there were a few with burgundy Bowie cuts, an earring and shaved-off eyebrows; and then there were some in short kimono-type tops and jeans doing the Carl Douglas dance to 'Kung Fu'... I couldn't believe my luck!

Then I started to meet Simon on a regular basis and he took me into Liverpool. I was intrigued – I was spending time with a man who bought Revlon hair products for his dry, damaged hair and foam self-tan.

About five miles from Port Sunlight, there was a place called Raby Mere, which is like some weird, remote bit of countryside, with a stream and some kind of really dense forest. Simon took me there one day – he had an airgun and he told me he was going to shoot ducks... something like that. It was great because I'd always wanted to go there; I'd never been there as a kid because I never had a bicycle.

It was a sunny country afternoon and then he just said, 'What if I shot you now if you didn't take your pants down?'

I suddenly thought, 'He's just going to shoot me – but he must really like me to do this, going to jail for murder.'

And so he raped me, he buggered me, but I thought, 'Well, this is how things go and it's surely not pleasant, because it's a bit like having a shit in reverse.'

It wasn't the best experience that I could ever have had. I was a bit shocked, but then I had had no sex education whatsoever – in those days, we didn't have. I was mortified when I heard the facts of life because I could not believe that my dad put his wee-wee in my mother's piss-piss, and it was really upsetting to think of that. They used to say 'bummer' at school about homosexuals, so I thought that you both went down with your bottoms – what other explanation could there be for 'bum boy'? So you don't automatically assume that your arsehole's going to get a dick up it, do you?

It wasn't brutal, although it was very painful. I thought, 'Oh God, I'm lost...' – I was a long way from home. There was nowhere to run. But *did* I want to run? I didn't really know what I wanted to do. So, I did what anybody with any curiosity and common sense would do and let him try and it was very painful. He drove me home and we didn't speak and I was actually more relieved to get driven because it was a very, very long way from home.

But I never, never regretted that. I think sometimes, unless society tells you something's wrong, you don't really know it's wrong. I was flashed at a lot by this poor retarded man in our village who was probably about 60 years old. He'd just pull his pants down and show me his dick; he did it to a lot of kids, but then I heard years later he had gone to jail for interfering with a kid. Now, if I'd thought it was wrong or knew it was deemed wrong by society and I'd said, 'Oh, that old man showed me his willy,' he'd have gone to jail a lot earlier. But I just saw a silly old man showing me his willy, so was it a trauma? No. I saw a willy. Had I gone to my mum and said that geezer had shown me his willy, she would have gone, 'He didn't show *me*.' But a normal mum would have gone, 'Oh my God, the pervert!' and 'It's wrong, it's wrong... oh my God, jail him!'

It was going to happen anyway, wasn't it, that I was going to get it up my bum. So I had to get home. Would he have shot me with an airgun? No, he wouldn't have. It was just that I'd never seen an air rifle before in the middle of nowhere, in a pair of 5-inch platforms and a clip-on earring, and Simon was big and strong. Later on, I replayed it over and over, and thought, 'Oh fucking hell, that really hurt,' and I thought I should have been upset about that. But I wasn't. And then I saw him again, although not in the same situation.

Simon held parties in this wonderful house. I was invited to go and stay the weekend and watch films. I went and stayed, and watched films, and there was no sexual activity whatsoever. He just said, 'Listen, I really love you and I'd like you to touch this,' and I touched it. Then he said, 'But, really, I'd like to put this there.'

And I was like, 'Oh no, it hurt last time.'

So he said, 'Well, what you do is, you go home and you get a toothbrush and you cover it in Vaseline and you sit in the bath and you insert the toothbrush and then eventually put one finger in, two fingers...'

I thought, 'Ohhh, I don't want to do that.'

But I stayed the Saturday night to the Sunday. I'd lied to my mum and dad and said I was going camping – well, I was in a way, wasn't I? – with a few friends and staying in a tent somewhere outside Chester and they were like, 'OK... as long as you're OK.'

Well, my friends went and called for me while I was away, so when I got home they knew I'd lied. But what was worse was that one of Simon's neighbours had seen me come out and had reported Simon to the police, because obviously he was queer because of his upmarket car and his new-look black hair. The police swooped and started to question me, because I'd been seen leaving Simon's house early in the morning, and the police were going to take me in for an anal examination.

My mum and dad didn't know what was going on, and I wanted to contact Simon but I couldn't. They were going to arrest him and wanted me to make a statement.

The police really put the pressure on me, saying I'd go to an approved school if my hymen was broken, although by this time I'd had toothbrushes and everything in it.

But one of my friends, Micky, knocked on the window when the police had gone and I somehow managed to scrawl a note: 'Go to Simon's workplace, warn him, say nothing'. Simon didn't know what was going on – he got this note, ditched it and, the next thing he knew, the police took him. They couldn't take him to a police station – they had to question him at home – and he just said, 'We watched films and we talked, and this is where he slept.'

Then I think Simon left his work. My dad was definitely mortified about the whole thing, but we didn't address the issue, even though my mum was, of course, was as liberal as they come – it was another excuse for alcoholism, because she was already a fully fledged sherry-head. As far as she was concerned, it was, 'Oh my God, my son's a prostitute, sleeping with older men...' and she really went off on one. And my dad's like, 'Look what you've done to your mother!'

I was confined to the house – I could not go out, point-blank, not to the city, and I was not allowed to leave the immediate vicinity. I don't know if that was a police curfew, but it was a definite curfew, none the less. So then I couldn't even take the train into Liverpool and that was really difficult, and Simon no longer drove past our house, and it was weird. I wasn't in prison but I couldn't leave the village or anything.

It's not like it put me off sex, because there was no sex – I didn't even give him a wank, and I didn't put his willy in my mouth. He showed me this great big thing that looked like a microphone and there was that one attempt and a half-attempt – 'Can I just try it?' 'Oh, maybe... Ooh – no!' Then there was the toothbrush lesson, then the one-finger, two-finger, three-finger shuffle and I wasn't going to do that because there was probably poo involved!

But I tell you what – it made me realise that a projected image opens doors, along with the door of George Henry Lee's department store. He seemed to have a lot of money, and I had Guerlain perfumes –L'Heure Bleue was one – and other trinkets that he'd buy me, such as Mary Quant's Make-up for Men kit.

Mary Quant launched the first make-up kit for men, which comprised a bronzer, blusher, a kohl pencil, lip gloss – he bought me those in several colours – the green corrective foundation, a bronze moisturiser... it was better than using my mum's or something that I stole from the local chemist. The kit cost quite a bit, and he bought me four of them.

He also took me to a boutique called Cape and he bought me a huge pair of canary-yellow, 1930s-style Oxford bags with turn-ups, and I thought, 'Simon's great!' He'd take me to clubs and I was meeting his friends, who were older and intellectual, and they knew a lot about a lot of things other than 'Wig Wam Bam' and the shit that was going on. They knew about books, and they knew about camp icons like Mae West, Bette Davis and so on, and it was just a complete banquet to me. And if the price to pay was one failed attempt that felt like a Chinese burn on my arsehole, it was so worth it!

People fall off buses and trip in the street, but I had a car on call. It was fantastic, and I could sit in that car with my feet up on the dashboard with the wind in my hair, gliding out of that village into the big city, and he even took me to Manchester! To me at the time, he might as well have been taking me to New York! I was 13, and could have passed for 20.

I wasn't calculated about it, though; it was cause and effect. I caused it subliminally and I got the effects, which were always, unquestionably, beneficial for a young boy who was a lot ahead of his time.

At school, if I asked Mr Ockenden, the gym teacher, whether I could be excused, he'd go, 'Yeah, go where you like... I'm not watching the clock.' So I'd leave school during the 15-minute break at 10.30am and not go back. I'd go to New Ferry, round the record shops and the comic shops and stuff like that, and think, 'That's it, that's done. Always go to Mr Ockenden, or Mr Griffiths.' I never did gym at school, never, because I was always so 'sick'. His diagnosis was a sprained ankle. He'd drive me home in his red sports car – I only lived 300 yards from the school! So I certainly got favours, and the adversity was far outweighed by the adult privileges.

Sooner or later, though, these childish fancies would have to end, and adulthood would slowly force itself upon me.

4
city slicker

'I do know that, when I went to acid house raves, most of the reason why people weren't aggressive to me was because they thought they were hallucinating. I was given diplomatic immunity because people thought I was part of a bad trip.'

I had to move out. I was in a village and I needed to be in a city... I *had* to get to a city. I was already going into Liverpool a lot at that time, and ending up at places like Virgin Records on Bold Street and swapping the price tags on album covers. At that time, everyone sat on the floor cross-legged, listing to stuff on headphones, but they were mostly hippies, a bit smelly.

There were so many albums I loved – the metal-covered version of Mama Cass's *Cass Elliot*; Peggy Lee's *Mirrors*; Buffy St Marie's *Best Of...* I adore Buffy St Marie.

There was another great album – *Elegy to Marilyn* by
Darien Spirit – with a picture of Marilyn Monroe on the
front with 3D lips that moved. Sometimes, I'd just buy
albums for the cover – that's why I got Buffy St Marie's
album, the double one with the red cover where it looks
like she's lying in the *kasbah* – I thought it was fabulous.
And there was Melanie's *Garden in the City*, that you
scratched and you got a waft of fragrance.

There was another great Melanie sleeve – *Stoneground
Words*... what a sleeve! It was a yellow cardboard sleeve
edged in heavy black fabric, and when you opened it
there was a sepia, full length photo of Melanie in a hand-
painted dress and a fan in her hand. And it came with a
fold-out of these beautiful photos of Melanie in the desert
in a burgundy kaftan with her guitar and sitting inside a
circle meditating. And there was a photo of her inside a
church, praying, with candles and stuff. You don't get
covers like that any more.

I thought Melanie was far more emotive a songwriter
than Joni Mitchell. Songs like 'Momma Momma', 'I Really
Loved Harold', 'Any Guy', 'Baby Guitar', 'Tuning My
Guitar' and 'Babe Rainbow'... they were just incredible. To
this day, they're major influences on me because, in many
of her songs, she could easily have been singing my life.
That hit – bang! – at about the age of 12 or 13.

Anyway, I was going into Liverpool dressed in a certain
way, because I had a sense of some kind of style. I'd send
for an Afghan coat through the *Disc & Music Echo*. I used
to go to Birkenhead market. My feet were far too small for

the stack-heeled shoes of that time, the 1970s, so I had to get girls' ones – I was only a size four and all those shoes were adult size. Later on, I'd see I had the very same high-heeled shoes as David Bowie – they were from Ravel for £4, but I got them at Birkenhead market for £1. There were a lot of second-hand shops in Rock Ferry and New Ferry, where I'd buy beaded 1930s ladies' swagger jackets, but they didn't look like ladies' to me. I remember I had a big checked wrap-over coat with a belt pulled tight, and some very, very wide trousers.

Whenever I went into Liverpool, I was aware of being noticed, but there was no threat, really. On one occasion, I wandered into St John's Precinct and there was a hair salon called A Cut Above the Rest. A few months earlier, I'd seen a *19* magazine that was dedicated to Biba and I'd come to London and I'd seen the salon – I'd sat there every day while I stayed with my brother, who lived in Acton. I used to travel into London on the train and sit in Biba – I'd no money, I was just a kid. At that time, I also saw *The Rocky Horror Picture Show* when Vivienne Westwood had done all the costumes, before it got commercialised. Little Nell was in it, along with various luminaries like Duggie Fields, Luciana Martinez de la Rosa, Andrew Logan... I didn't know then, but I think I was there on the second night to see *The Rocky Horror Picture Show* and, believe me, it wasn't what you see now – some clown in suspenders and an old lady's wig on. When it first started, it was Vivienne Westwood biker jackets and torn-up stockings – it was punk.

So I'd seen that and Biba, and in St John's Precinct there was this salon – dark brown, peacock feathers, art deco – and I looked through the window and thought, 'I'll be a hairdresser.' So I went in and asked if there were any jobs.

I think they took me for a lot older than my 14 years. That's when I first clapped eyes – and my heart – on Lynne. She came to the counter; I remember her hair – she had hair like Mary Travers from the folk group Peter, Paul & Mary, but in the deepest henna red, and a green dress. Something must have clicked with them, because they gave me a Saturday job. I lasted precisely one Saturday, because they would shout, 'Pink!' 'Blue!' referring to the rollers, and I was saying, 'What's the fucking difference?!' I didn't know what the difference in the size of a roller was – no one told me, I was just straight on the job.

Later, I'd walk past in the Precinct and think, 'Fuck, you really blew that one.' But Lynne was like, 'Oh, hi, Pete!' and I got to hang out with Lynne in Herbert's Café and she'd buy me lunch. If I could get the fare into Liverpool, which was 13 pence, I'd go and walk about for a while and then it was, 'Oh, I'm on my break in 15 minutes.'

Soon, Lynne started to take me into work and show me how to shampoo, but I wasn't salaried and I had to get out before the owner came in. Then I was gradually introduced to the owner and, before you knew it, I was there full time.

Bowie was big then, as was Bryan Ferry, and I was

buying clothes in Rock Ferry that were way above anything you could get in Anne Twacky's then, so I had arrived, cooked. I was going to see Roxy Music – 'Love Is the Drug' – and Lynne was decked out from Bus Stop. There was a Biba make-up counter in Dorothy Perkins but, hold on, Birkenhead market had all the Biba make-up because Biba had shut down by then. There was the blue blusher, the green lipstick, the yellow foundation and the pots. Dorothy Perkins didn't have the more extreme version because its range had been watered down for the conservative clientele. Then, suddenly, Biba stuff appeared in Rock Ferry in second-hand shops and I'd take it into A Cut Above the Rest and sell them the stuff I'd bought for five shillings, and it was just fab.

When I'd gone to stay with my brother in London in the Biba days, there was a shop called Let It Rock, and one day I heard this sound blasting out – a scream, a Little Richard song. I went in there and, to a kid like me, it was fab. It was rock 'n' roll and Biba.

I used to get *19* and *Honey* magazine – oh, God, I'd love those issues back, particularly the Biba one, which was a whole issue. I got one and there was this piece on Acme Attractions – the clothes stall in the King's Road that later moved into a shop and became Boy – and there was a little article in it, headed, 'JORDAN COMES TO TOWN', accompanied by a picture of Jordan – the self-styled punkette and Vivienne Westwood devotee – on a train platform in Brighton with a very demure Log handbag, that beehive and a vinyl, buckle-flap crotch leotard with fishnets with these great muscley legs – really looking ladylike walking down the platform. Buried in the article was an address where she worked.

Lever Brothers at the time were running an offer with soap powder – save the packet tops and get two nights in a London hotel and a train ticket. So Lynne and I sent off for the tickets, and we came down and we had £22 each. We ended up in a nice hotel in St John's Wood, where we dressed up to the nines, got the tube to Sloane Square, and we walked and we walked and we walked… we asked people about where we could find Jordan, and this girl at Acme Attractions said, 'Oh, you don't want to go there… there's nothing in there.'

It was a hot day and we were tired, but I said, 'No, we've got to go.'

So we walked and walked, and Lynne was in heels and she wasn't too happy. We got to the corner and we thought it must have gone and then we saw that pink foam sign – Sex – and the doors were blacked out with black rubber curtains. I just pushed that door and I was in Narnia. Hank Mizell's 'Jungle Rock' was on a loop and it was so loud! There was this statue at the end, and it was the most amazing statue I'd ever seen. Suddenly, the statue moved and it said, 'Hi! Can I help you?' It was Jordan wearing a T-shirt with 'Venus' written on it, with bits of bike tyre and human hair.

She walked towards us and the floor rumbled – she was only tiny but she was kind of big. She was whiter than white and she had tiny little black gloves on and these really great plastic trousers with a lot of buckle detail, the Venus T-shirt with all the tufts of human hair, this silver beehive that no photo has ever captured, and those black stripes on her eyes that went into her hair. Then the newsreader Reginald Bosanquet tried to come in! Reginald Bosanquet! It was amazing.

I bought a T-shirt with a dirty story on and some plastic trousers, and Lynne got a rubber skirt and some kind of see-through mesh top with a dog collar. And Jordan was like, 'Why don't you guys come and see the Pistols tonight? We're doing this big party...' and we were like, 'We can't – we've got to go home!'

'Oh, I can get you guys somewhere to stay,' she said. 'You know Sue Catwoman?'

'Yeah,' we said in unison. We'd never heard of her!

But we would come back as often as we could. We stayed in squats in Shepherd's Bush and we got Giros because we were unemployed and we'd starve and save – and it was just to look at Jordan. If we were there for a few days, we'd wait mid-King's Road and she'd arrive kind of late, because she was coming from Brighton – it was a two-hour journey and the shop would open whenever she felt like it. And you'd see this person coming down the King's Road. Sometimes it wasn't a pornographic look – she did an Elizabeth I style once with red contact lenses. Just *seeing* her you'd think, 'Well, how can I go in there today?' But she became very friendly with us and we were sort of adopted.

Once, we came to London to visit Sex during

December – me, my friend Paul Rutherford and Lynne. We'd saved up all of our pennies for this event, thinking we were going to wow the world at Christmas. So we trudged down the King's Road on a snowy day, freezing cold in our fishnets and vinyl, turned the corner to 430 King's Road – and what do you know? It was shut.

As we were standing outside, somebody with a clipboard came up to us and said, 'Hey, we're doing this show with the Sex Pistols tonight called the *Bill Grundy Show*. Will you guys be on it?'

We said, 'Oh yeah, yeah.'

'Well, could we pick you up at like 4.30pm?'

'Yeah, yeah,' we said, but we got distracted – we got lost in the King's Road and then went to Harrods – and by the time we found a phone box it was too late. They said, 'The car can't find you,' so we thought, 'Fuck it – let's go home.'

But do you know what we went to Harrods for? The same foundation that Jordan wore, by somebody called Alexandra de Markov. There was an interview with Jordan in the *Sunday Times*, in which there was the usual 'Hair by Ricky Burns; Eyeliner by Max Factor; Foundation by Alexandra de Markov exclusively at Harrods', so we had to get a bottle of what Jordan had. It was £17 – our entire budget – but we knew that that was the fountain from which Jordan drank.

Then I realised – those flesh-coloured rubber stockings – you could buy them from a catalogue you got from the *Daily Express*. That's what Westwood was doing – buying fetish wear from some company in the north of England and putting it on the street. I didn't know it was fetish wear – it was just a great look. So I was wearing that during the day and, the next thing I knew, I wasn't allowed on the Port Sunlight train, because that had come from Chester and people were freaking out at nine in the morning.

I'd got the bike-tyre T-shirt – I think it was £11 and that was a big investment. I was wearing rubberwear and Lynne was wearing rubber skirts, rubber bras and 5-inch heels. I also remember the hairdressers giving me written warnings about my clothes. We were told eventually that we were not allowed to work on a Saturday because the security guards in the Precinct couldn't control the crowds that had come to see me and Lynne through the window. All the other staff were in Biba and Bus Stop and wearing dark make-up, and we were ghost-white and Lynne had her hair done in a salon that specialised in 1960s hair, wash and set, and thick eyeliner. I had a jet-black quiff, flesh-coloured rubber stockings and pink high-heels, the bike-tyre T-shirt and little gloves. My dad then decided to intervene, and wrote a letter to British Rail. They said, 'OK – we'll give him a first-class carriage.' I heard later that Jordan had experienced the same thing from Brighton – they put her in a first-class carriage.

But it all changed after Bill Grundy was on. On the following Sunday, everything was on the front of the tabloids, particularly Jordan as Punky Pam, who planned to stay in bed for Christmas, eat bananas and who knew what other punk disorder? That gave people a label. Punks had been identified, they were foul-mouthed and aggressive.

Suddenly, all of us were in danger. By the time I left work the night after the *Bill Grundy Show*, people were shouting, 'You punk filth!' and I was getting jostled and shoved. And then somebody hurled a bottle at the train compartment window. And then the first-class carriage was allocated a security guard. I found myself in a first-class carriage with a security guard totally to myself, because now people felt it was open season to beat up a punk. Suddenly I wasn't even a queer, because I couldn't even get in gay clubs, so I was a punk.

The strange thing was, we were treated like VIPs, so it prepared me for pop stardom on some level, because I was causing a commotion and so was Lynne. I remember Lynne going to work in a black 1960s polo-neck sweater with gym knickers and big hefty suspenders with stockings that were just a little bit too short so her thigh bulged over them – it was all calculated. It was all set off with thick eyeliner, black gloves and round-toed high-heels. The effect it was having on people! We didn't know the sexual connotations, because even the words 'homosexual', 'sado-masochist', 'paedophile'... weren't around then. The new word now for me was 'transvestite', but did they call David Bowie a transvestite? No. Nobody knew what a transvestite was. So there's always a new label.

Then Lynne came to Port Sunlight and my mum

virtually had a seizure. Lynne saw my mum for a while, and then she said, 'You can't stay here.' And she just took me to live at her house, at 50 Wells Street, Kensington. Her mum and dad, her auntie Ann and her brother John all lived there, and I had the sitting room, the parlour. I just lived there and we went to work every morning and came home every night and ate things like chips and gala slice from Marks & Spencer. Then we started to take sick days and we'd go to the cinema, and we had our dreams. And all of our dreams really did come true.

Dressing up wasn't to construct a cocoon around myself, but it worked as a cocoon. I knew no other way. It was just what I knew and I didn't know it was wrong. There were these images, I guess, and the clothes were really available because no one else wanted them. People say I must have known when I got dressed up like that that I was going to attract attention. No! I knew I was being noticed, but I wasn't intelligent enough then. No one said anything. To this day, no one will tell me I look nice, even when I know I do. I know the effect I have on people now. But no one will say you look great or fab, so in those days there was nothing to be said either.

Whatever anyone has ever said of me, whatever they have called me, you cannot say I lived a lie. I put on the clothes I want because they are my second skin. I pull them on even if I am in the house on my own all day doing the vacuuming. It is not an act for me; it *is* me. And it was me back then as well, even though it was hard.

Walking through the Liverpool streets in full Vivienne

Westwood regalia in the late 1970s and early 1980s was no party. And that wasn't all I did. I got black contact lenses. I painted on black nails or whatever the hell colour I wanted. I had huge extensions in my hair – black, red, whatever. Plaits, bunches, whatever.

Particularly in the teenage years, I was pushing the edge of being downright offensive in people's eyes. It was just an adventure and I was playing around with imagery. It's fashion now but in 1977 it was a political statement and I was very much involved in that movement of using visuals. It wasn't consciously to offend – I just started to realise that, when people are confronted by something on such a level, they can't deal with it. I can remember once wearing a see-through plastic mac with just a G-string underneath – and no one would look at me! In a picture, it would be considered offensive, but, if you were actually in front of their eyes, they were speechless.

It's like Leigh Bowery and the way he used to look. He'd think nothing of painting his face and body in outrageous colours, with the most intricate make-up, huge eyelashes and thick clown-sized lips. People very rarely said anything. He'd go into straight clubs nude with lightbulbs in his hair or a merkin on. That was the effect I was having. I didn't have much respect for Leigh Bowery – he only did it in nightclubs. I did it from morning 'til night.

People wonder how many nightclubs I went to. I never went to any; I went to Eric's, which has closed now. I went to a few gay clubs but we got barred because of the way we dressed. There were a few hotels in Liverpool that ran a Bowie night but I wasn't going to wear Bowie trousers then. I'd gone beyond Bowie. I was doing Vivienne Westwood and Vivienne Westwood shut the door on David Bowie when Sex was up and running. She even locked Mick Jagger out in the Sex days – 'No… Go away!' Jordan slammed the door.

And, yes, I got hassle. Of course I got hassle. And that in itself taught me a lot about myself, and about the people who jeered and jostled. For me, I think it taught me I was strong enough. On those streets, I could face down a group of youths with Stanley knives and I could survive. I could face down old women who wanted to hit me with their umbrellas because my very presence affronted them. I suppose they'd have preferred the streets to be full of the youths with the knives.

What it all ultimately taught me about the real freaks, the ones doing the shouting and giving the hassle, was just as important. It taught me why they shouted, why they jeered. When they do this, it's never really about me – it's about them. Whatever I'm wearing, it's not me they're seeing. It's themselves. A well-buried fear, a secret desire. 'Look at him… what a freak!' is what they think they're saying. 'Look at me, I'm here, too,' is what I'm hearing. The louder they shout, the more they want the world to look at them. It's almost like a competition for attention, a primal jealousy. And don't try shouting me down as a drama queen who craves attention. I don't dress or look the way I do to get attention. If anything, I did it to build walls and to fend off attention. I do it to stop people approaching me, to keep me as isolated as I was back in Port Sunlight as a child.

Later, I used to walk from my flat at 59 Catharine Street in a Vivienne Westwood white loincloth, rags in my hair, a pirate jacket and the strappy boots that I've still got. I'd be invisible all the way down Church Street; I'd cross that road and, by the time I got to the alley, I was on the home run. No one had said anything because, I realise now, they were too shocked. There was silence where I walked in Liverpool. They were dumbstruck.

Courtney Love – who was in Liverpool then – hung out outside Probe Records. She'd often be out there after the night before, with a mouth on her that could stop a train. What a woman... what a life. She was a wild, wild girl. She brought LSD to Liverpool in a huge carrier bag and she was responsible for the whole change of the musical climate in Liverpool, due to her distribution of Superman LSD tabs which Julian and the Bunnymen and all of that crowd were dropping and going on a transcendental Jim Morrison experience. I was far from wild – I was living with Lynne's parents, on my way to getting married – but there were times when Courtney found herself in my shadow... or, at least, that's the way she perceived it.

There was always a sense of foreboding when I approached Mathew Street. I loved the mornings when I could stride into Probe without hearing her screeches. Remember that TV series *The Magic Boomerang*? Well, she was the one who brought everything back to reality. Even when I invested in a Sony Walkman and turned BowWowWow's *C30, C60, C90 Go!* album up to full blast, her voice could still penetrate the headphones and I'd think, 'Uh oh, she's off!'... 'HEY! FAGGOT! ROOSTER!' She had a piercing voice, so I didn't want to be noticed by her. I just didn't want her to draw other people's attention to me when I got on the home run of Mathew Street.

Yes, sometimes she'd throw a Coke can, too, but, hey, she was a bad shot. What I realise now about Courtney Love is that she'd got fire inside her. I'll see her sometimes on TV – she's so intelligent and articulate. She's a genius, or, at least, she was then. So all she was trying to say was, 'Hey – I'm here, too!' That's what people mean when they shout at you in the street. 'Faggot!' 'Queer!' 'Transvestite!' ... all they're trying to say is, 'I'm here, too!'

I didn't know her, but I got to know her a bit some time later – I met her at the VH1 Fashion Awards and I know someone who works for her. And I know she's in trouble, but, when you're that raw and that intelligent, sometimes you have to try and slow yourself down, and you do that with drugs. It's like when a baby throws a rattle across the room and screams because it can't communicate. Courtney Love's got that. And she's dangerous, because she knows a lot about the music industry, politics and hypocrisy, and she could have a voice. And people don't want a voice like that. So she's shouting into a vacuum, and the inevitable result is the drugs and the drink and the rehabs and the violence.

But let's not let this get out of hand. I did read in a book that she'd hit me on the head with a plant pot or something at a wedding, but that wedding never took place. And if she *had* hit me on the head with a plant pot, she'd be dust!

Some people have said my looks at this time were always quite threatening – and still are – but that all depends on their perspective. The black contact lenses – why were they threatening? It was like the Little Prince statue. They were beautiful, those black contact lenses. There was never any ugliness about it. I didn't have blood dripping out of the corner of my mouth and a tomahawk through my head. How do you perceive beauty? Beauty is in the eye of the beholder. My message is – behold yourself. I thought that every image I did at the time was beautiful. I *worked* on those images. It was a gradual progression, like the half-yellow forehead with big dreadlocks, and the hair was shaved at the side and painted. Then there was the complete white face and white eyelashes with the black lenses. It's very organic to me.

I've been looking at fashion magazines – I like the editorial because it usually makes me laugh – you've got to wear this or you're not worth the steam on someone's shit – but everything I see now Vivienne Westwood invented. I get the magazines for the scrapbook for when I'm dead but I can't even look in a clothes shop other than Westwood. I go and look in Westwood and it's pieces of art. It's all so well done. It stands alone. If you don't get it, you shouldn't have it. It's not something you can get because there's an explanation – it's intuitive.

But threatening? What is threatening? What am I supposed to do? Wear a little frill? Some people have said that a threatening look might be a kind of defence. So I'm a shy, retiring little flower and I just do this to keep people away? Please don't go down that route. If I wasn't doing this, I would still be the same way. There's no way I'd think it's time to wipe it all off, or tone it all down and get a job in a bank.

What is a defence? Is keeping your wallet in your pocket when you walk down the street a defence? Is locking your front door a defence? Aren't we all, to some degree, taking defensive steps? It's a jungle out there. It's not a defence – I'm not scared of anyone or anything. Defence to me would be having a gun or a knife in my bag. I don't need them.

I'm an exclusive members club, and those who understand get in. To those who get me, it's intuitive. They don't ask me those questions and there's no need to answer them. You know, sometimes you see a doorway and you're scared to walk through it, and then other people see the same doorway and they march through without a second thought. I'm that doorway that a lot of people are scared to walk through. It's like me walking into Sex – it was very intimidating, but I walked through it. I am that doorway. When people see me, I believe they see themselves – I'm their mirror, but what they see is what they bury in drink and drugs and food and compulsive shopping. Everyone is burying something. I feel very naked. No matter how much I put on top, I feel very naked – you can see it all.

Do I think males should dress up more? If they *want* to. You mustn't hide. You'd be surprised, because, if you like yourself, people like you right back. But, you see, I've always had diplomatic immunity in that area, because people let me put on a show – and they always have. We all have animal intuition or, shall we say, a spiritual sense, and I think the majority of people know it's right for me, and that's the way I am. And it's not just since *Big Brother* – there's been very little hostility towards me. I've always walked everywhere and I think high visibility causes indifference and ultimately acceptance. It goes from 'Jesus!' to 'Oh, here's that fruit!' and then it's 'Oh, hi, Pete,' and finally 'Oh no, not him again.'

5

labelled

'Gay to me conjures up a moustache, a check shirt and doing twirls to Gloria Gaynor records, and, if that's what gay is, then, no, I'm not gay. I'm not side-stepping any questions – I go with both.'

It wasn't long before we got fired from A Cut Above the Rest – we got three written warnings. So then, under Dad's advice, I went to several doctors, and got sick notes for nervous conditions, during which time I started to source second-hand clothes. Then the salon decided they didn't want us back because, if we were suffering from nervous disorders, we weren't stable enough to do a perm. Dad had steered it that way and we took them to an industrial tribunal, because if you win you get compensation and you automatically qualify for benefits. We got maybe a few thousand.

Another reason we were fired from the hair salon was because Jayne, our receptionist, felt very threatened by Lynne and my rubber clothes. She was nicknamed 'Kojayne', the bald girl, in clothes from Bus Stop, and she was in one of the tabloids as 'the bald woman of Liverpool'. But then we turned up in fetish clothes, and Lynne in her big high hairdo, and she was threatened, because, as the receptionist, she was the front of that salon. So she went to the boss, whom she was living with, and made sure that we were pushed out. And then Jayne emerged in Big in Japan.

So then we sourced fun fur – shocking-pink spiky fur – and Lynne used to make sweaters out of it. They looked like Wombles suits in shocking pink and black. Then we took those to London and wholesaled them to Acme Attractions in Chelsea Market. We sold a lot of those for £15 a pop and they were £3 to make! We then got chair legs and with them we knitted string with patches of mohair, and we sold these string cardigans to Vivienne Westwood for £15 each. Lynne also knitted mohair sweaters, dropping stitches and leaving pieces hanging off so they'd go out of shape. They became a punk staple – we couldn't produce enough of them.

We rented a big room in Casey Street next door to Minsky's, on the fourth floor, so we had to climb a lot of stairs. I went out sourcing our materials beyond Lime Street – the Jew Shop, it was called. It was run by two old Jewish people who stank, with a smelly dog, but they had tons of the winkle-pickers from the 1960s – crocodile skin

– I bought them for £1 a pair. They also had plastic macs with moving pictures of the Beatles on them.

Then I had an idea. I looked in the phone book for rag merchants. Liverpool's a sea port... they have links to China... *cheongsams*! So I went to a rag yard and bought all I could. I couldn't buy it all, so I wore a baggy coat and stole a lot. They were all put on sale in Casey Street, and every punk was in that building on a Saturday. The money was flying, but it was crazy, because we also lived there, too.

Then the Sex Pistols came to town. It wasn't in Eric's – it was in a place round the corner they'd hired for the occasion, a 'one night only' thing. John Lydon took me into the dressing room. He was adorable. Everyone claims to have been there, but they weren't – it was empty. There was me, Lynne and Paul Rutherford, Pete Wylie and a few student hippies – but anyone else who says they were there, they weren't. They didn't know a Sex Pistol from a water pistol. They thought Aretha's something you sent to a funeral – or they did then.

But I was with the Pistols and Jordan and they saw my clothes. They said, 'Come to London and sell these clothes to Acme Attractions.' So we'd go back to Sex, or Seditionaries, as it later became.

The Casey Street lease ran out but Geoff Davies of Probe Records came in – he bought a load of fur jumpers and an Anarchy shirt. He was like, 'Fuck! This is really happening!' He then said, 'We've got a room in the back of the shop – you can have it.'

'We can't afford the rent,' we said.

'No – we want you in the room, the back room of Probe.'

It was on Mathew Street, right in the heart of Liverpool. The shop was like a padded cell. We got bin-liners and opened them and stapled them to the ceiling and the walls, so it was like a patent-leather padded cell. And we had a crimson plastic floor and pink polythene over all the windows.

Probe Records was wonderful. A lot of the time, the kind of people who go to places like that are dreamers – people like my brother Tony, maybe, who dream about making music while spending hours looking at records made by everyone else. Nothing wrong with dreaming, but what set Probe apart was the fact that so many of the dreamers in our padded cave didn't stay that way. It was a strange and talented community, customers and staff alike – those who passed through included people like Pete Wylie (Wah!), Ian McCulloch (Echo & The Bunnymen) and Julian Cope (The Teardrop Explodes). It was a vinyl-filled hot-house.

But I wasn't as much a part of it as most people thought. I was behind the counter, but only because it was boring staying in the clothes shop in the back and I could play a lot of records that I'd never get the chance to hear otherwise. I wasn't actually working there – Geoff just said, 'Come behind the counter. You don't need to know the alphabet – we'll give you £50 a day and just use you as an ornament.' And then he asked Lynne, too, because she was wearing crinolene – Victorian stuff – and he said, 'Wear bigger ones!' Geoff was fab.

So I wasn't in the heart of the Liverpool music crowd. I listened, I joined in some of the conversations, but my mind was still on clothes. We went to the Army & Navy stores and bought an awful lot of old army clothes. We went to Lynne's house, filled the bath with black dye and Parker ink, dipped them, but never rinsed them. Lynne sewed straps on, while I glued things on.

We were doing pretty well. From a tenner or so a week at A Cut Above the Rest, we were making hundreds of pounds in good weeks. One night on television, Billy Idol and Generation X were performing, and two of the group were wearing clothes they had bought from us. It didn't *mean* anything, but it was good to see it.

When Lynne and I weren't working at the back of Probe, there was one other place we went – Eric's, on Mathew Street. Eric's was set up by Roger Eagle, Ken Testi and Pete Fulwell. It was a private members' club, which meant it could stay open 'til 2.00am, amazing in those pre-alcopop days. The Stranglers played on its opening night in 1976 and, from then on, the list included everyone from Blondie, Generation X, The Clash, Ultravox, The Jam, The Police, the Sex Pistols, and all the Liverpool names who would be part of everything – Orchestral Manoeuvres in the Dark (OMD), Echo & The Bunnymen, The Teardrop Explodes and Wah!. They were all there, along with all the people from Probe and all the other hangouts.

What helped give the place its atmosphere, and prompted queues all the way down Mathew Street, was the fact that it was never a money-making machine for the owners. You could see a band for £1.50 some nights – or 50 pence in the one-of-a-kind afternoon shows. Eric's was about the music and the people. They even set up a record label, fanzines and other magazines. They built a whole world. According to Roger, there were about 5,000 people on the club's membership lists at its peak, and there was a big banner-waving protest march through the streets when it was raided by the police and closed down in the early 1980s. They did two huge raids on Eric's and I was there on both occasions. They were pulling people out by their hair. They confiscated my dog collars, my wristbands and my high-heeled shoes because they had studs on. They said they were an offensive weapon. They put me in a van but they didn't actually arrest me because I just got out of the van and walked off.

It's easy to say that Eric's was the Cavern Club of its day. But while it was unique, and it spawned some fantastic music, it wasn't anything special to Lynne and me. It was just the place we went, where we felt at home. In those days, there was a hardcore of about 100 who were there night after night, gig after gig. That was me, Lynne and 98 other people.

Who came to Eric's? A lot of pub bands who wore stripy pyjamas and called themselves punk. There weren't many. The Damned did nothing for me. But Roger was one of the few promoters booking American bands at a time when British bands were taking over. Americans had entranced me as a boy in Port Sunlight, when all I had had were album covers and occasional TV performances to watch. The Americans blew me away as a teenager in Liverpool when I could finally see them up close. What got me was the show, their bravery and their brazenness. It was broader, deeper, more alive than the political things the British bands were obsessed with. These bands were the ones pushing boundaries, I thought. Which was why I felt the need to follow them.

So gig after gig, I was there in the front row, which wasn't difficult as many of the gigs were half-empty, because all the other fans preferred the British bands. I got backstage as well. I was in their dressing rooms, waiting in the wings, sitting in their vans, living their lives. It was like I had been adopted. And never, not since I'd been a child watching my mother put her make-up on at dawn, had I ever felt so protected. I had been lifted into their world and, for some reason, these big older stars wanted to put their arms around me and protect me. I've had guardian angels all my life.

And then in Sex – the shop – some pictures appeared on the wall. A few months before, there had been a *Melody Maker* cover of this creature with a big white hairdo with 'The Dave Clark Five' forming part of this structure on its head, doing the most fabulous pose. It was Wayne County, who'd been signed by MainMan and had recorded an album called *Queenage Baby* that was due out, for which Bowie wrote 'Rebel Rebel'. The next thing

I knew, there was a sign outside Eric's saying 'Wayne County & The Electric Chairs'. I said, 'Lynne... that's the one we saw on the *Melody Maker*!'

We got there at five o'clock, and there was this balding man in the dressing room.

Lynne said, 'Where's Wayne? Where's Wayne?'

'I'm right over here, honey.'

And she gasped, because we didn't know what a drag queen was. We had no clue. And Roger Eagle was like, 'This is the Lenny Bruce of rock 'n' roll!' And we stared at this shy elderly man. (I know his real age, but I would never reveal it – I can't count that high.) There we were, in the thick of it; we spent *days* with Wayne County & the Electric Chairs.

An amazing transformation overcame Wayne County on stage – and it certainly wasn't feminine! He didn't wear drag then. He'd come to England wearing an army thing with a beret and Dietrich make-up, with stitches on his face. I was wearing an awful lot of make-up, too, but his was of a different calibre, and it certainly didn't look female to me. It was total self-transformation because, by the time he'd finished, he looked like Dietrich. He had to dampen it down a lot for Safari – lose the lashes and the stitches – because he did this beautiful Hollywood face with really authentic stitches as though he'd been cut.

The punks went mad for him! He was doing 'You Make Me Cream in My Jeans' and the Rolling Stones' 'The Last Time', and he'd go into that trance thing –

'Rock 'n' Roll Resurrection' – and beat his head in the drum kit and pull the beret off and his make-up would come off. Then, afterwards, he'd be like, 'Oh hi, honey!' He didn't even swear.

After him came Johnny Thunders & the Heartbreakers with 'Chinese Rocks', and with them they brought the volume and their attitude, and they were American, wonderfully American. I fundamentally believe I've got an American soul. I love them, because they're so enthusiastic about the new, because they have no cultural history. They haven't got Queen Victoria and Elizabeth I and they're just so basic. They fly to the moon, stick a flag in it and call it theirs.

When I went to London, I found myself staying with Wayne County & the Electric Chairs in a squat. It was fantastic – it was huge and there were all these people coming and going, like Siouxsie Sioux, and we had to pretend to be very sophisticated. They weren't 'stars' – we were just taken into their world. We weren't awestruck – they were just people who seemed to have a life that we had no idea really existed. Cocaine was around. Sometimes it was offered on a big plate – it looked just like icing sugar. We just said, 'No thanks, we've just had some.' We didn't know what it was! We just knew it was something you put up your nose.

All this went on for years with the Heartbreakers, and then David Johansen came on the scene, and Iggy Pop – I was blown away.

The track that I loved most at that time was The

Strangeloves' 'The Night-Time Is the Right Time' from 1966, and guess who started their set with it, and still does to this day? Wayne – now Jayne – County, with a ten-minute intro and all those slide guitars and the atmosphere builds and then he comes on – 'I hate the day!' It's almost like watching some kind of preacher. And it fitted the look, one that could only exist in the dark.

It was also of a sub-culture I didn't know – the transsexual thing. We didn't know what they were, but it seemed to me exotic nightbirds. Things do look better at night, and people change at night – people spend more money at night, they drink more at night. The moon is a very powerful force on people – there's something magical about night-time. Image-wise, what I would like to have conveyed then through my immature set of pretensions was the night-time, that I was a night-time person. The Four Seasons sang *'And the night begins to turn your head around...'* What a great song! So everything I liked revolved around night-time. Yet, there I was, up at eight in the morning!

Then Roger Eagle told me that I couldn't come back to Eric's until I'd formed a band. His exact words were, 'You get a fuckin' band together.'

'I don't want to be in a band,' I said. The thought appalled me.

'You're gonna get in a fuckin' band or you're not getting in the club.'

'But I don't know anybody!' I said.

'Right! Next Friday! I've got you a band next Friday!'

So what could I do? I couldn't go to the club and now I couldn't go to The Bear's Paw gay club across the car park from Eric's – 'No, we don't let the punks in.' Previous to that we'd been referred to as the Bowie crowd. So I had nowhere to go at night, and it was six o'clock bed for me on Saturday nights and Thursday nights.

I'd never even thought of performing – I just wanted to have my clothes shop. I just wanted the money so I could buy more clothes and go down to London and look at Jordan. That was all I wanted. And then I wanted a flat – preferably in the King's Road – so I could see Jordan coming to town.

I did think of moving to Brighton, because that's where she lived. At that time, when the norm was Jerry Hall in the *Siren* days, it was Jordan's look and her sheer presence that blew me away. It was all very well done – it wasn't messy. There's a bit on *So It Goes* with Tony Wilson when she throws a chair, and you can just make out a swastika armband. She was only 19 then, and she spoke so sophisticatedly and was clearly very well educated. But when you saw her in the daytime, and the body – I'd never seen anything like it in my life.

So Roger Eagle formed the group for me. He picked the musicians and stuck me in front of them and I had to take it from there.

Julian Cope was a student at Liverpool Poly. Pete Wylie was a mouth about town – I didn't really know much about him. We rehearsed for about a week in Julian's flat with Roger Eagle, and I just had a broom. He said, 'You've got to learn to use a mike stand.' I didn't even have a mike – I only got it on the night. Julian and Wylie had amps, and Phil Hurst was the drummer. And going through these records with Julian – 'Sympathy for the Devil', 'Walking the Dog', Iggy Pop's 'I Wanna Be Your Dog', The Move's 'Fire Brigade', Manfred Mann's 'Doo Wah Diddy Diddy', which was Julian's idea and I hated it. We called ourselves The Mystery Girls, which came from a song by the New York Dolls, whose clothes had been designed by Vivienne Westwood.

Our first gig was on 4 November 1977 at Eric's, supporting Sham 69, who attracted a mostly skinhead audience. I was wearing a black leather polo-neck with buckles up the back, Nancy Sinatra go-go boots with a tiny little heel – inspired by the Russ Meyer film *Faster Pussycat Kill! Kill!* – and black leather gloves. And my hair was in a plasticised Elvis thing – I used to pour liquid plastic on it and dye it with ink. I topped it all off with lime-green contact lenses, and a big, thick, black leather dog lead which I used to clip on my ear.

When I came on, I sensed such energy off the audience... and there was a load of other stuff coming off the audience as well – cans and glasses and plastic bottles. The skinheads didn't know how to react so they thought with their Heineken cans. But they didn't hit me, and it just inspired me to keep going. We were so defiant that Phil Hurst just carried on playing for 15 minutes once we'd left the stage after 'Sympathy for the Devil'. I thought that was so fantastic.

So how did my first stage appearance feel? I'd played to a packed house – I'd seen other groups play to about 16 people – and I felt I'd really cut my teeth. I could handle a mike stand and I could really sing. And that was it – I'd done it.

We split up the next day. It had been intended as a week but I just couldn't see the point. It may have had something to do with Julian deciding that I had to stand behind the drum kit with a fire blanket on me – he was going to stand at the front and Wylie would wear a toilet seat on his head. They thought it would be a great idea if the singer wasn't seen. 'Let's do a reverse thing and put the drummer at the front.' Try and work that one out. I think they thought they were going to try and sell it to me as a kind of Bauhaus arts project. That was enough for me.

The big night did change how others saw me, though. I performed with The Malchix – and then I got fired after one song. I only ever really wanted to go to clubs, stand at the side of the stage and do one number. By then, Adam & the Ants had appeared, and Jordan used to come on and do one number called 'Lou' – just scream her head off with all that red paint – and then walk off and pick up her handbag. So I thought, 'That's what I want to do!' I didn't want to sweat it for 45 minutes, so I had it worked out – arrive, stand at the side, then, halfway through, wake them all up... and go!

I rehearsed with Big in Japan for a while and we did a great set, and then the producer Noddy Knowler was doing a compilation album for Open Eye Records and he asked me to contribute; he asked Ian Broudie and Clive Langer to do a track with me but then they gave it to Jeanette Landry and Lori Larty. Ian Broudie told me at the time, 'Look, they're stars... you've got nothing.' Several times I started to work with Ian Broudie and even Dave Balfe, and then on the day we were going to do something, they'd say, 'We've changed our minds – you just can't sing.'

Then, in August 1978, a revelation – I saw *Top of the Pops* and some man was on, and then a fan was fluttered across and then it was a woman, 'You make me feel (Mighty Real)'. And I thought, 'God, isn't that great?' I was riveted; I'd seen Sylvester for the first time.

We used to travel quite a bit then – to Manchester to see Wayne County, or to Wigan where I saw Slaughter & the Dogs. It was the only way you could get a group of people together. We couldn't get into a gay club, so what else were we going to do? We'd finish work in our shop, we were dressed up and we'd think, 'OK, it's Saturday night... where can we go? We'll go to Wigan.' We'd hang out all night and then we'd get the train back in the morning. And always Sylvester was coming on.

I knew he'd played in London, with John Lydon and Siouxsie in the crowd, and in Eric's the DJs always played his 'Mighty Real' and 'Dance (Disco Heat)' alongside 'Anarchy in the UK' and 'New Rose', and the floor was filled. So Sylvester's stuff... that was the music I wanted to make. All I wanted was music with a 'wobbler' on – that was the only word I knew for it – I didn't know about sequencers then. If I was going to make music, then it would have to have a wobbler on.

And so Nightmares in Wax, my new band, came together in Eric's. We latched on to Martin Healey, because he was really middle-class and he turned up in a blazer with 'Sod the Jubilee' written all over it – like really normal clothes that he'd splashed a bit of powder paint on, and would then make sure it was cleaned off before his mum saw it. He'd come in the clothes shop and he had the same sick, black sense of humour as me. We saved up and bought a keyboard in Hessy's in Whitechapel for £200 and, I have to say, it was the most crashing disappointment.

This might sound incredibly naive, but Marty and I thought you got one, switched it on and it went 'dugga-dugga-dugga-dugga-dugga-dugga ... zrooooop!' Marty would switch it on and it would go, 'Zeeeeeew...' and make all these noises, but he couldn't programme it and he was pounding away with two fingers! We didn't know how this music was made, and nor did Noddy Knowler, or any of those people. Then later, after we'd signed our record deal, I said I wanted to sound a certain way vocally. I naturally assumed that I'd immediately go in front of the microphone and I'd have a falsetto just like Sylvester's. And it was one of the biggest shocks that I was obviously a tenor or a baritone. I kept asking if they had any 'tweakers' to make me a falsetto singer or any pills I could take to do it. I was mortified that I couldn't sing falsetto!

I wanted the name of the band to be Sex and Violence, but the rest of the group vetoed that. I thought we could do the *Captain Scarlet* theme and go *'Sex and violence...'* I was just having some fun, you know? But Nightmares in Wax was Roger's name.

I also wanted to make a disco record – that's what 'Black Leather' was supposed to be. I only used a four-track studio, Amazon Studios, but it came out and it did really quite well. But then I was asked to do some shows, and we only had those tracks – the three on the EP. I did 'Automatic Lover' as well, but that never got released, because obviously it was about a vibrator. Someone also asked us to do a radio session, so John Keenan from the F Club in Leeds and the Futurama Festival came. We didn't have any songs, so we ended up doing Simon Dupree & the Big Sound's 'Kites' for ten minutes!

The single just kept selling, so I did the rounds of the radio sessions and the F Club and then Manchester and colleges – and they were huge! Then we hired a place called Kirklands, which had an upstairs room, and we'd sell out. All that money for a few fly-posts! But, however well things were going, I couldn't live with that name, Nightmares in Wax. The Cramps took me on board, because they thought we were all going to be into all that, but I just thought it was awful. It's like Heinz – it's just a label.

What next? There was a period when I got a flat in Catharine Street and I was still doing the clothes shop but the radio sessions died off. Then we were booked on *So It*

Goes to do 'Flowers' and we needed a name fast. I had a book called *Those Who Died Young*, but the guitarist at the time said his mother would throw him out if he was in a band called that. So I said, 'What are we going to do?'

'Wanted: Dead or Alive!' he said.

It seemed so dramatic, I was like, 'Whatever, OK.' And, after that, I was everywhere. I never ran after it – it kind of ran after me.

People have said 'Flowers' was gloomy and not very like Sylvester, but I didn't have a sequencer, did I? I was just thrown on the stage – I had to do something! If someone kicks you out from the wings, what are you going to do – cower in the corner? You sing streams of shit. We just had one cover after another and a load of shite that streamed together. We never had anything written down – I just ad-libbed. But, if you kept your face straight, people thought it was style. I liked 'San Francisco' but, at this time, Doors albums were flying round while there was still Echo & the Bunnymen, and I thought, 'Oh quick – best hop on that one.'

I know I've been compared to Jim Morrison vocally, but I never listened to them. The Doors track I was aware of was 'The Alabama Song'. I love the bass line on that one. And 'Roadhouse Blues', I like that one. But, as for 'Light My Fire', I preferred Nico at that time, but I wasn't ever going to pull it off as a German chanteuse with a harmonium, was I? When we did the Futurama Festival, Nico was on the next stage and she was still playing when we started off with 'Misty Circles'. It was exactly the same as before it was released, but we then had a sequencer and we were gonna use it! I remember Nico storming into the back room – 'No one does that to Nico!' Well, I just did...

Then I got better people, like Wayne Hussey, and various outcasts. I seemed to attract the most talented but unlikely musicians, like a guy called Mick Reid, who was a bit of a Keith Richards clone and just never stopped playing his guitar on full volume.

Wayne Hussey was fabulously talented. He'd been in a group with somebody called Ambrose who'd worked with a group called Hambi & the Dance who were in the Ananda Marga religious sect, and I happened to be rehearsing at his place in Lark Lane among some of its followers. It's an Indian religious cult, a bit like the Krishnas but with petrol – they set fire to themselves for religious causes. The in-joke was that, if he got to Number One, he'd go on stage at *Top of the Pops* and pour petrol over his head and burn himself alive, which I thought was really fabulous. I went and bought all his records in dozens. I just thought it'd be so great if Hambi went on stage and set himself on fire – what a great *Top of the Pops* that would be! But I mean that in the best possible taste!

Soon, we'd made our own 12-inches and we got a publishing deal for 'It's Been Hours Now'; it seemed like a lot of money because we didn't have a record deal. A photographer called Francesco Mollina came in to manage us, and he was fantastic, but the press said, 'Aagh, we're not ready for this.' That was around the time of the New Romantics, and I wasn't romantic and I definitely wasn't new. A brave, new, trail-blazing trend that turned music and fashion upside down? My arse! It was basically dreamed up in some dungeon in Covent Garden run by Steve Strange, dressing up like a bunch of twats in tablecloths and lampshades. What was that about? It was pantomime, as though Vivienne Westwood had a few weeks off and they had to find something to wear on their own.

I was the real thing then, and, when Rough Trade suddenly jumped at 'It's Been Hours Now' and it went huge, the gigs got bigger. We had our own label and offices in Bold Street with an assistant called Doreen Allen. Things were definitely on the up.

6

abstinence makes the heart grow fonder

'When I'm called a "freak" by the 3am Girls, I think it's highly complimentary, especially when I look at them – a bottle of shampoo and some Clearasil wouldn't go amiss in their case.'

Around the summer of 1977, I began my first non-sexual relationship with a guy. At the time, there were the Spitfire Boys – Paul Rutherford and Budgie – and there was Big in Japan. And on the stage with Big in Japan was this man wearing a gypsy bandana, with beaded hair and a tuxedo, with a fan, just standing to one side. He was older than the others, and it turned out to be Griff, the bass player in the Spitfire Boys. Big in Japan used to use him as a stage presence, and he seemed very sophisticated. There was no sex with Griff, but he was very much my mentor at that time.

He travelled with me when Lynne was doing other things, because Lynne and I weren't in an actual relationship at that time – it was just starting. I couldn't get into gay clubs so I hadn't come to terms with that. I'd had one previous sexual experience, but that had been forced upon me.

But Griff became a mentor and I remember going to stay with him all week; he had all the Sylvester albums, and all the Lou Reed and New York Dolls albums. He also had an alter ego called Caspian, which involved him dressing up in a tuxedo, greasing back his hair and being terribly sophisticated. He had another alter ego which was a bit like Gene Kelly in that movie where they sing 'New York, New York'. And then he'd just be Griff, the punky guy. I think he was about 38 or 40 – I'm not sure – but he must have seen something in me.

Griff lived in Arundel Avenue, in a lovely flat with two girls, Pat and Liz. He didn't work – his job was being. Nobody needed any money during the punk era, because you got your Giro. It was about creativity.

We used to go to the Armadillo Rooms, and we'd look in 69a, a place for vintage clothing, that sort of thing. We basically lived a café society lifestyle. We were always in the Armadillo Rooms for lunch, then we'd sit there all afternoon with a coffee, and then we'd go to see the bands at Eric's. Then someone would go to the university, so we'd go there. Then Griff and I would go to Manchester. We went out every night, really. It was winter – my favourite time of the year – and I remember walking up

Princess Avenue in the snow. Griff taught me to drink, and we'd get hammered on snakebites (cider and lager).

He introduced me to Warhol – *A to B and Back Again* – and *Ciao, Manhattan*, the Edie Sedgwick movie. He introduced me to *Chelsea Girls*, and this great live double album by Lou Reed – *Take No Prisoners*. There were books, too, a lot of books. In the afternoon, we'd go to Philipson & Nephew and he'd take loads of great books – William Burroughs and stuff – but he wasn't impressed by them. He didn't wander around saying, 'Ooooh – this is great!' He'd say, in a very refined way, 'Oh, can you *believe* this? And people are using this as a sort of behavioural code? They want to be Jack Kerouac.'

Griff was a quiet man, had a great sense of humour and could be very pretentious with other people if he wanted to be. He'd watch them going along with it because they thought it was for real. Like when he was Caspian, he wore the smoking jacket with the greased-back hair – very Rudolph Valentino – but he did it well because he was older. He'd hold his head in a different way and he'd talk in a different voice, and you'd see people who'd seen him earlier as a different character start to respond to this one. We used to get back to the flat and laugh so hard.

We'd get invited to big Sunday dinners – there was Arthur Black and that whole set, The Moderates, an arts band. They did 'Tulips from Amsterdam' and they used to get this lady out of a mental asylum, Dame Looney, she was called, and she did a long version – probably over an hour – of 'Mull of Kintyre' – '*Oh Mull of Kintyre, oh mist* rolling into a… Mull of Kintyre, oh mist rolling into a… Mull of Kintyre' – they were the only two phrases she knew. She wore crocheted hot pants, a pair of clogs and smelled of urine. She'd talk like Pam Ayres and she used to think Jimmy Savile was talking to her through the TV. People thought it was a bit cruel, but it was entertaining none the less. There was a huge line-up – Clive Langer and the Deaf School set, Bette Bright – and it was all based at the Everyman Theatre on a Saturday.

There'd also be these dinner parties at 12 o'clock on a Sunday. Someone would have everyone over to a big rambling flat on Princess Avenue or Huskisson Street. It wasn't unusual for it to be painted black and there'd be a nice portrait of Marlene Dietrich on the wall, and we'd have something on in the background like Dietrich, Lotte Lenya, Edith Piaf or a Kurt Weill thing. There'd be just an old table with woodworm, a beautiful piece of fabric thrown over it, a great big old dish and someone would have poured chocolate all over the grapes. Someone would spray an old broken chair gold – really badly. It all looked so right. It wasn't decaying splendour, it was just spot on. And there was Rive Gauche perfume sprayed everywhere.

What about the guests? There was Jayne Casey of Big in Japan with her head shaved completely bald with a big butterfly stuck on the side, black lipstick and a pencil skirt and a corset – she looked like a shop mannequin with the wig removed. I'd be in a black polo-neck sweater and vinyl trousers, with stiletto boots and black gloves – I always wore little black gloves – and a really white blank face. There was Lynne – no photograph from that time has ever captured what Lynne looked like because we were all gurning in them – she had this huge, teased-up, jet-black, kiss-curled hairdo and polo-neck leotard, with gloves and a belt, and thick black tights with white stilettos. Griff looked like Johnny Depp in *Pirates of the Caribbean*, but with a really gorgeous vintage suit.

Arthur Black was this older guy who'd have an entire German Reich day on a Sunday, when he'd play the speeches of Hitler and march up and down in a Nazi uniform for hours. People would go round and we'd drink calvados and we'd watch Arthur doing his stuff. There were no drugs – we didn't know what drugs were. But it was cool to do what you wanted and be what you wanted and say what you wanted – as long as you weren't a mess.

Because no one had any money, we'd have Asti Spumanti from Marks & Spencer in champagne glasses. We'd dye the mashed potato blue with colouring, and hard-boiled eggs were dyed pink with Jelly Tots. I don't know what we were doing, really, but it was very civilised. Someone would have a trampoline in the garden, so we'd have a trampolining contest on a Sunday afternoon. Our Sundays were just *great*. I was in with the older boys and girls. I wasn't *aspiring* to be more sophisticated, because they wouldn't have let me in. And I didn't try and get in – they pulled me in.

Sunday was the best day, because by that time Eric's had started to wane. We'd run out of bands. What had happened in music then? We didn't know. I think at that time music hit an all-time low. There was only one good record at that time – 'Behind the Groove' by Teena Marie. But that was in the punk clubs. We didn't see *Top of the Pops* because Thursday was the big night at Eric's. So we didn't know the mainstream – I think disco was big at the time, so that was in the gay club, which was across the way from Eric's. We went and knocked there and they wouldn't let us in because we were wearing offensive weapons – razor blades, which were blunted – so we thought, 'Up yours.' So it was Saturday night, watch a late movie in Lynne's parents' front room, and then get up on Sunday at 10.00am and then go to Arthur Black's.

How many of my newfound friends did I sleep with? None. And, if they wanted to sleep with me, I wasn't reading the signals. It was a time of ambiguous sexuality, when people just slept with people, but it wasn't a time of promiscuity. We were all too young. Sex now has become so readily available; there's so much written about it and so much spoken about it and there's such an obsession with it – at that time, it just wasn't talked about or indulged in to the same degree.

I almost looked on sex as a journey – I had something to give and I hadn't found the person to give it to. I lost my virginity to Lynne. That was truly the first fully rounded sexual experience I'd ever had, and that was a very, very frightening prospect. Oh, God – we went to see *The Exorcist* and we were both scared shitless – so we fucked! And it was a bit like *The Exorcist*, I guess! It was just a new sensation. A tickly, woozy, messy sensation and it happened, and it continued to happen. I couldn't believe that this bit down below was doing something that wasn't hurting my bum. It was very vanilla!

Then, in August 1980, we decided to get married – how conventional is that? And why not? Sometimes, old traditions are just the right thing to do, and we thought we'd do it. She bought the licence – she paid £7.50 for me, so that was good value.

On the morning, we rolled up at the Register Office and, when the registrar came in, he just said, 'Which one's the bride?' which caused a guffaw of laughter. So I said I was and he said, 'Cheeky!' They had to interrupt the ceremony halfway through because dustbin lorries were making a racket outside, but it was over in a flash, and off we went.

Lynne had food poisoning from the previous night and I vacuumed the flat. We didn't want any of that wedding reception crap – people drunk and making speeches. We just wanted to get it done and, besides, it was long before the age of selling it to those glossy magazines for an inordinate amount of money. What celebrities did I know then, anyway? Ian McCulloch? I don't think so!

I'd say, shortly after we were married, maybe a year, we stopped having sex. As somebody who is the active one sexually in a male–female relationship, I associated it psychologically with hurting somebody, because the idea of somebody making a noise – whether or not they reached orgasm – meant I must have been hurting her. So it just died – we didn't have sex from then on. But it was fine. Love is not about sex, and sex isn't love. But, if you get the two things combined, it's quite a miraculous thing. So she didn't have any dalliances and nor did I.

The divorce has been horrendous, but it wasn't a big mistake. Lynne was there at every gig and on every tour. We left together every night.

I did sleep with men, but I didn't have sexual relationships with them. I seemed to be drawn largely towards totally impotent men, but I never thought for one minute that it was me causing that impotence. 'Thank Christ for that – we can go to sleep!' And they didn't want anything but to have me there.

So I guess I was a bit like a concubine, because I did look great and I was pretty and I did have a good body. And Mum was always naked – in German families it seems to be inherent – so I was quite uninhibited then. Inhibition came some time later. I'm sure people have this impression through seeing my performances and the energy I give off that I'm some kind of tacky old queen who gives blow-jobs to taxi drivers for a free ride home. Well, it ain't like that. I conduct myself with a lot of self-respect and dignity.

And what about drugs? Surely I must have been tempted? People are too busy wasting themselves now – it's all far too hedonistic. I've tried speed, but it was terrible – I called it the 'awful sulphate'. I thought it was going to eat my face from the inside! So no more of that. At first, it had been great because I sold records all day and I was very enthusiastic about everything and we'd walk home babbling. But afterwards, it was horrible – you'd feel all dry. So that was it for me and drugs. Nada in the larder!

7

taking a hit

'I hate people thinking they own part of you and, once you've had a hit, some people think they can do what the hell they like – pulling your hair out, yanking you out of vans – and you're not supposed to react.'

In 1982, Island Records were interested in me, but they wanted demos, and we weren't going to do demos. Danny Goodwin, who'd signed Boy George to Virgin, came up to see me at a club in Liverpool and it was packed. He elbowed his way in and said, 'Look, if you start to lose some serious weight, we'll consider signing you.' So I didn't want to go and meet with Virgin, because they already had Boy George, although they did offer us a deal through Francesco, our manager.

Then Epic came to see me at Heaven. I had decided not

to do showcases; to me, that's like being a prostitute and giving a free fuck away to see if they come back next time and pay! I was doing my gigs and getting paid and, if they came, they bought a ticket as well.

I was in a good place. I had a publishing deal – I didn't want more. I was living in a housing-association flat at 59 Catharine Street for £6 a week and it was lovely. I was doing these shows and I could work behind the counter in Probe two or three days a week. We also had the universities and I could hire Kirklands or the State Ballroom. It was all I wanted, so what did I want that they could offer me? I had fame in a weird way, so all they could do was amplify what I already had.

But Epic came to see me at Heaven – I was wearing the G-string and long rubber gloves, and I already had 'Misty Circles' and a couple of other tracks. There was nothing I wanted, but they came up with something like a ten-album deal. We wanted a long-term deal, for more than a handful of singles and a launch album. We wanted time to develop and grow, and even then it wasn't easy to find a record company who would let you. So I do feel sorry for artists today who get even less time and have to sell their arses to score a first hit. Musical development? Not any more.

The first advance was £35,000, which was a lot to me then. It made me feel like a millionaire. And we had total artistic freedom. So we signed to Epic in the summer of 1982. But then the goalposts moved. Epic's A&R people – Muff Winwood and Annie Roseberry – well, words fail me. They wanted Culture Club; I wanted Bobby O, who'd done Divine's 'Native Love'. They wanted a ballad; I wanted 'Native Love'. Then they decided they wanted Altered Images; I wanted to alter my image. Oh, fuck!

First, we went to Martin Rushent's engineer – Tim Palmer – and did 'Misty Circles'. He got it – fantastic. We were only given 24 hours to do the whole single and mix it in Genetic Studios, so we were in on Friday morning and left on Saturday morning, and went straight back to Liverpool. We were cooked. We thought, 'Yeah! We've done a real record and it's all metallic and it goes chugga-chugga-chugga-chugga!'

But Epic said, 'No – it's got to be re-recorded.'

We were going to use Patrick Cowley and Two Tons O'Fun, Sylvester's ample backing singers, but they needed four plane seats between the two of them.

So Epic told us, 'We've got this other guy who's done this amazing band called Fashion.'

It turned out to be a German guy called Zeus B; I met him and he played me Gina X's 'No GDM' – the Quentin Crisp thing, 'no great dark man' – and she sounded like Dietrich gone disco. Zeus and I spoke a lot in German and he got it.

So then we came to London to record *Sophisticated Boom Boom* with Zeus. We stayed in a beautiful flat in Maida Vale and I just about thought I'd died and gone to heaven. We had £10 a day each from Epic and we used to save half to go to Vivienne Westwood and buy clothes. Zeus and Tim Palmer were so fab – they were the happiest days of my life. I could get strings, I could get the girls who did backing vocals for Scritti Politti and I could get a brass section – oh, it was such a joy to wake up every day and go to that studio.

Zeus B Held and George Galloway, my housemate on *Big Brother*, are the best people I've ever encountered. What can I say? I remember Zeus describing the sounds of a sequencer – 'Sounds like boiling eggs, *ja?*' And he told me once that he'd got a demand. 'I have zis demand from the veird tea man.'

'What weird tea man?'

'The *veird tea man!*' He meant the VAT man. He was so great, Zeus. He was my favourite ever to work with. There was just joy, and laughter. And we kept the record company out of the studio at all times. They were never allowed in.

One unexpected event was that we lost Wayne Hussey. He was a Mormon then, adhering very strictly to the Mormon religion, but he was such a lovely person. I loved Wayne. He was fundamentally a very important part of the block, but our sound was getting so much more synthesised, so there was very little room for Wayne's guitar. Then Tim Lever, the keyboard player, came in white-faced one day and he gave me Wayne's book – it wasn't a diary; it was a lyric book and notes. He'd written things like, 'I hate being in this band... The music's not fit for anything other than a drunken lurch on the dance floor... When am I going to express myself? Perhaps if Pete dies, I'll get to be the front man.'

I was really upset, and Wayne said, 'I'll just leave then.' So he left my group, grew his hair and wore a dress! How great is that?

We were lacking a song; I had wanted to do 'Play That Funky Music, White Boy' but we did 'Black Leather' instead. I didn't even like the song! I was just ad-libbing that track. But it was great to record – there was a brass section added and it sounded funny, and it soon became a single.

When I'm recording, I usually start off with a cover and usually it doesn't go on the album, but I bounce off the track just to get the dust off. Then I'll bounce from that track to the rest. Then the record company hear the tape and they hear a cover and they get silly.

Well, you can sign for total control but, if the record company don't agree with it, they just won't market it. So it was a process of letting us have our way and doing nothing to assist it, then showing us, if we did it their way, it would be a guaranteed sure-fire hit. I knew this straight away but, on principle, I wanted my songs released, because they were really important to me. First there was 'Misty Circles', and then the follow-up was 'What I Want'. That was so important to me, but they wouldn't do a video for it.

Then came 'I'd Do Anything', and they decided they would do a video. Then they tried to pull it on the morning of shooting, but Tim Pope, the director, forced it ahead. It was a great track but no one would show the video because I was wearing black contact lenses and I had a huge live panther in it. It was a great scene but they wouldn't show the animal. I was hours with this huge panther called Bella on a set on my own, surrounded by guns – a great experience! I was trying to recreate the Roxy Music *For Your Pleasure* album cover on a shoestring budget, and the record company were just like, 'Whoa, no way, honey, no way.'

So we reduced the black contact lenses shot and took the panther out, but suddenly the MTV programmers said there was a man with female breasts pulling his jacket open and they couldn't have a transsexual on MTV. The suit comes open in the video and it's very visibly a male chest, but they decided it was a female breast. And, when we proved it wasn't a female breast, I had a make-up smudge on my suit and they objected to that. And that was the end of that – *finito*.

After that, Epic reissued 'What I Want' with a massive fly-posting campaign but it still wasn't a hit. So then they did what they'd waited for all along – they got all the buttons in place and did 'That's the Way I Like It'. And guess what? It charted. It got to Number 22 in March 1984, but then *Top of the Pops* went on strike for the first time in its history, and it went down. And, when I did get on, they didn't like what I wore – the record company or *Top of the Pops*. It was a yellow bodysuit by Westwood but the producer at the time said I had a cricket bat down the front of it and I had to tone it down – it was wobbling.

'Well, tell the camera man to stop filming it then!' I told them.

Did having a hit change my life? Well, it wasn't really a hit, was it? Number 22 and out! It went down, then I was on *Top of the Pops* and it went down further. So nothing really happened. All that changed was that I was on the cover of all the music papers. I was on the cover of *Melody Maker* and photographed for *Smash Hits* and things like that. And we were in the London Metropole Hotel, which was a step up from the Columbia Hotel. We used to come down on the Thursday and stay at the Columbia 'til the Monday, then come back on the Thursday, and that was fine for me.

Mike Percy, the bass player, and Tim Lever, the keyboard player – they'd be at the bar with ABC and people like that, but I used to go to bed. I was reading a lot, and I was out during the day. It may sound pretentious, but I'm telling the truth here. If you're getting out at eight in the morning, you gotta get your look on, get your free breakfast, then you're in a taxi to the studio in St John's Wood. We'd stay in the studio 'til midnight, taxi back to the Columbia at two, in bed by three, up at eight. It was great. We got £10 a day living expenses and you could very easily eat spaghetti carbonara for £3 in an Italian restaurant round the corner, so you'd save the money and buy more clothes. That's the way it was.

Was I happy with *Sophisticated Boom Boom*? It was an event. There were no gaps, that was the most important thing to me. It was all hard metal and, the next thing you know, New Order were sounding remarkably similar.

Production and sound – it was great, yeah, but song-wise, no. 'What I Want' was great; I still start sets with the 12-inch version. That song to me – the whole sound of the sequencers and all the reverses on the vocals and the big note – that was a one-take, there were no drop-ins on that. Zeus was like, 'God... you can sing!' and he was so into it. 'I'd Do Anything' was just fantastic. I don't think I'll ever top those two pieces of work, especially the lyrical sophistication of 'I'd Do Anything'. If I died, they'd be what I'd want to be remembered for.

Again, it was all about sound and vision. Some of the ad campaigns that we ran were just genius. I was the best rodeo prize anyone could ever win, all dressed up in a pair of skin-tight leopardskin pants. We took a lot of old 1950s movies, or 1950s postcards, and we just had a great hoot with me in a skin-tight leopardskin suit with the hair over one eye and the leopards and things. I thought, 'Let's run with this!' I'm not sorry for a damn thing I did, but I did think somebody somewhere would think, 'This guy's got a really good sense of humour.'

Did I get grief for going from indie to disco? If we did, I didn't hear it. There are so many opinions, aren't there? Did I read all the music papers and look for a good review? No. I was marginalised by my peers, like the Bunnymen and The Teardrop Explodes, but then what did I want to know them for? I had Marty and I had Geoff, and I had Lynne and Griff and Paul Rutherford, so what did I need all those other people for? To me, they were Jim Morrison wannabes, and who'd want to be some old hippie who died a fat slob, drunk in a bathtub? Jim Morrison means absolutely nothing to me.

The first time I heard Divine's single 'Native Love', I stopped dead. I just fell on the floor. I wanted that sound so badly. I dug and dug and found that his work was produced by somebody called Bobby O, so he was who I wanted to produce for me. That was how I was going to create great music. Epic didn't want us to work with him – and they certainly weren't going to pay us to go to America to do it.

Back at home, I was listening to music and trying to work out what to do. Lynne and I had a radio alarm clock next to our bed, and it was almost always on. It was on that that I heard two songs that spoke to me. The first came from Hazell Dean. 'Wherever I Go (Whatever I Do)' had the polish and the production value I craved. I sat on the bed, motionless, trying to piece together how it was done. Then I heard Divine's new single 'You Think You're a Man'. Again, I pretty much froze in the bedroom. It didn't sound as good as 'Native Love', but it was still fabulous, still the kind of music I wanted to make.

So I investigated and found out that Bobby O hadn't done this one. Some other people in London had – some guys called Mike Stock, Matt Aitken and Pete Waterman. We tracked them down and I met Pete first. He was up for it. But the record company – the people who'd signed me – were hardly enthusiastic, right to the point where I had to take out a bank loan for £2,500 to record 'You Spin Me Round (Like a Record)'.

Clive Langer was the main producer Epic wanted – he heard 'Spin Me' and said it was awful. Winwood seemed to know Pete Waterman, as everybody does, but it was 'No – he's not a producer... not Stock Aitken Waterman', so there was all of that going on.

At that time, I'd brought management on board whom the record company had said not to use, so, of course, I chose him. That was the Chris Morrison Organisation and Chris Morrison jumped on 'Spin Me' and arranged a bank loan for me from the NatWest Student Bank in Liverpool to record it.

Pete Waterman said we'd got a Number One, so we got going – and, for all the nonsense that has been said, for everything that might have been done differently, those times in London were magical. We were still hungry; we were still fighting. We had no real money, no proper budget. You want a sandwich for lunch? Fuck off – we still can't afford it. But what we did have was a new desire to take it all on again, the studio equipment and the song. And we had three wonderful people to work with – Mike Stock, Matt Aitken and Pete Waterman.

So we did two days' recording. We'd done a recording in Amazon Studios in Liverpool, but they just turned it off and taught us how to repeat the first verse, record it once and just edit it.

Then the record company said it was awful. It was unanimous – it was awful, it was rubbish. And they were still farming round for other producers – Rick James, George Clinton... it was all so wrong, so wrong. Then they said we weren't going to do an album – 'because Pete Waterman's not a producer and... er... if it's a hit, then we'll do an album'. Muff Winwood's last words were: 'Well, if this is a hit, we've got an album full of hits. If it's not a hit, we've got an album that's a waste of time. But can we not have a picture of him on the cover?'

They never wanted me on the covers. Then he wouldn't do a video, so we ended up paying for it. I'm not exaggerating any of this – these are the bare facts of what actually happened.

How did I write 'Spin Me'? I listened to Luther Vandross's 'I Wanted Your Love'. It's not the same chord structure, but then that's the way I make music – I hear something and I sing another tune over it. I didn't sit and study the Luther Vandross album – I heard the song and it locked. But, if I can't play an instrument, what am I going to do? I'm trying to structure the music and I know what I want. I can't play a damn thing and I don't want to. It's like do this, do this, do this – and suddenly it hits. I don't want to do Luther Vandross's song, but I can still sing the same pattern over it.

And there was another record, by Little Nell, called 'See You 'Round Like a Record' – she'd made another great kitsch single in the 1970s called 'Stilettos and Lipstick'. Fabulous – they were like Phil Spector records. So I had those two, Van Dross and Little Nell and – bingo! – done deal.

And it was a hit – so all of a sudden we had about three weeks to record an album. *Youthquake* was shit, but the remixes were great – 'My Heart Goes Bang', and 'Lover Come Back' was a good song, but then listen to the album – it's crap. Pete Waterman's approach was: 'Get a single and then we'll remix,' and he was right, because, when we remixed the songs later for singles, they were great. As an album, it was dire, but it's in a great package – Mario Testino's first non-fashion photograph – so it's a shite delight, isn't it?

'You Spin Me Round (Like a Record)' got into the *Guinness Book of World Records* for the longest time any single had taken to get to Number One, ending on 9 March 1985. What did getting to the top mean? First of all, it was a complete shock. I got a phone call saying that it was Number One. I thought it would have gone down by then. I just remember being in the flat that morning, feeling a little fragile, and Chris Morrison saying, 'You're Number One.' I remember Steve – my drummer and then manager – going, 'Whooo...whoo... whoo... whaaaaa... that's fantastic!' but I just felt sick, because I knew everything was going to change. The minute that chart was on Radio One, I left the flat to go Marks & Spencer.

And the hostility! I went to the Armadillo Rooms and the whole time people just looked at the table. I heard a gang of mobsters were planning to break into the flat and rob our millions, and these were serious Liverpool gangsters. I went to get a taxi later that week, and a gang of schoolgirls came running at me. I thought, 'Oh, autographs...' but they were kicking the taxi, saying, 'Get out of Liverpool!' It was all very hostile. I'd be called 'The shame of Liverpool, you piece of fucking filth!' It was hatred. I mean *real* hatred.

I'd been invisible up 'til then, and accepted like a mythical creature – a unicorn – that you'd see from time to time in town. But then I was Number One and people were really angry, especially the people I'd moved among, the musicians. It was like I'd done a shit in the Vatican.

And then I was on planes, awful flights out of Speke Airport at 6.00am with horrible coffee and sausages that were like widow's memories. I'd arrive in London and be straight on another plane to Germany. And I'd get to Germany and I'd feel sick, but I'd go out and do the number and I'd have to stand on a mocked-up record for the chorus, and they'd spin the wretched thing while I'm trying to sing and the equipment would go flying all over the place. Alternatively, on European shows, I'd just go and sing the record and 15 people would come on dressed as Liquorice Allsorts.

Then all these people wanted to work with me, people I'd never heard of. It was as though someone had taken the blindfold off and, in another country, I was fabulous and adored and revered, and then I was in Sweden and Belgium, where it all went mad because of the video, and then I just went 'STOP!'

In Liverpool, I think I could be accepted while I was the underdog, a bit like being disabled. I think there was tolerance for me because those people at that time probably related to me as the underprivileged kid. But once I was up there... I was living on the park, I had a flat in a purpose-built block and it was gorgeous, with a balcony and everything, and I thought I'd arrived – until I got in the top five and then I had to get out. And now I'm going through the same thing all over again.

8

holding on

'When you are in a job where you achieve a level of fame, people don't allow you to grow up and change your mind. Something you say on a Tuesday might not be what you think on a Friday, but, once it's down in print, it's there for ever.'

I didn't dream as big as Lynne. Lynne always knew we'd live on Holland Park Avenue in London. When we were doing *Top of the Pops*, even with 'That's the Way I Like It' or we went down to do something, we'd drive past Holland Park Avenue. I remember when I was doing *Mad, Bad and Dangerous to Know*, we had to move to London, but I'd already bought a flat in Liverpool. She said, 'Holland Park Avenue,' and I remember being very tense and going, 'You stupid bitch... we're never going to live on Holland Park Avenue.' It's an expensive area to buy in and I couldn't go looking because I was recording this album. The next thing I knew, she'd come back with a two-bedroom maisonette on Holland Park Avenue, and Elvis Costello was living on the floor above.

My accountants, who worked at my management team, faffed and didn't want us to buy it – they wanted us to buy somewhere more expensive, so I was in debt and kept working. But Lynne went in and said, 'This is what we want,' and we got it. So I got a mortgage and I bought my dream home in Holland Park Avenue. I couldn't believe I could buy a flat for £125,000, and it was the most beautiful home I've ever had.

Working in America had always been my dream. As I've said already, American artists had burst into my teenage world, a mass of colour, confidence and endless sunshine. American music and American production values were what got me up in the morning and kept me awake at night. Kylie, Jason and Sonia were moving in on the UK charts, and I wanted out. I wanted to go west, so touring in America was set to be the biggest and the best thing I had done.

When 'That's the Way I Like It' became a hit in the States, our record company flew us over there. Pop star glamour, excitement, luxury – you'd expect that, wouldn't you? Well, what the fuck went wrong? We weren't in a private jet; we were flown on People's Express – it was like being on a fucking bus and the fare was about the same.

As it turned out, that crappy journey was going to be the high point of the trip. The good side of it was that we were a good gang, out there. As well as the band, there was Lynne, of course, and a group of friends from Liverpool who'd joined us pretty much under their own steam. But none of us got the chance to have much fun. The Empire State Building and the Statue of Liberty could have been on the moon for all we saw of them.

The itinerary was as tough as it could have been. Interview after interview; talk after talk. Every radio station from every hick town between there and LA seemed to be on the list. Every dumb question you never wanted asked was an opening gambit. We worked it, because that's what we were there to do. But it cost us. We had big gigs to do, but, by the time those moments came, my voice had gone, lost down the line to all those radio stations or left in the air-con on the Sardine Express. So I let myself get pumped up with cortisone and steroids to get through the set. And, while the audience was hot, some of the execs were cold. Everyone was demanding things. Getting from show to show, interview to interview, meeting to endless meeting was chaos. And I was just too fiery for their taste.

In our down-time, I think things were happening too fast for me to focus. We saw a pretty early Madonna gig, in which she writhed away on a bed like a woman possessed. But it passed me by. Andy Warhol was there, someone who's a hero of mine now. But at the time? I just saw him as a stupid old man in a wig, so we didn't connect. And now we'll never get the chance, which I will regret for ever. Was it too much, too soon? In a way it must have been... and we'd not seen anything yet.

Back in the UK, I started the album *Mad, Bad and Dangerous to Know* with Stock Aitken Waterman, and everything was going OK, but they were getting very, very busy and going off in another direction. Despite that, it was wonderful and I was going from the Westbury Hotel to moving into a flat and, in 1986, 'Brand New Lover' went big in America. I was very proud of that, because we'd got cellos on it and a flamenco guitarist.

And then we were asked on the *Basil Brush Show*. I complied with that. I came straight from Germany, and I was wearing a stetson because my hair was filthy. The producer told me to take it off but I refused and we argued back and forth about it. I almost walked out. But I did the song and then he said, 'Right, you're going to be interviewed by Basil Brush now.'

'I'm *not* talking to a puppet,' I said.

'Oh yes you will!'

I'd had enough. I left.

Despite it all, 'Something in My House' still got to Number 12 in January 1987, but I was told I couldn't wear the black contact lenses to do it on *Top of the Pops* by one of the BBC people. The record company weren't happy with the black contact lenses either – the record company weren't happy with anything – but then nor was *Razzmatazz*. When I wore the black contact lenses and a black polo-neck for 'Something in My House', they put an effect on so you couldn't see me and quickly switched to Mel & Kim.

It was at the beginning of 1987 that my mother got

cancer. The day after she was diagnosed, she did a photo shoot with me, and you know what? My mum was still a professional. Her appearance came first, even when she told us she had lung cancer and that the doctors were giving her just four weeks to live. She'd got the news the day before, up in Clatterbridge Hospital, the same place where she'd given birth to me. She'd gone there because she'd had back pain after a fall in the kitchen a long time ago, but she'd ignored it. She'd put up with it for a long time, but then she realised it might be something else. She was right.

We were due to do a photo-shoot for the *Mail on Sunday*'s *You* magazine the day after Mum had told us her news. And we went through with it because she told us to. She was in it as well and the show was going to go on. I was crying at times, when the cameras were on us. So was Lynne. So was my dad. But there were no tears from Eva. She was immaculate, ram-rod straight, smile in place, make-up perfect, because she was on show and she was damned if she was letting anyone see inside of her.

And then the phone call came – 'You're on the Who's That Girl? tour with Madonna!'

No one had even mentioned it, but my manager, Chris Morrison, phoned me up. 'We wanted to keep it as a surprise for you.'

'My mum's got lung cancer,' I told him, 'she's got four weeks to live!'

'Oh, I'm sorry, but... you know... anyway, they're

going to make sure the record goes double platinum! They're gonna buy advertising, merchandising...'

'Chris,' I said, 'I can't do it. I can't do it!'

Then, like a twit, I ran up and down Harley Street with an open cheque book. 'Please cure her! Have everything I've got!' I was prescribed a medication called Ativan.

'Will this cure her?' I asked.

'No,' I was told, 'but it will help you get through it.'

Ativan is a heavy-duty tranquilliser, and I said, 'I don't a need a tranquilliser – I need some hands-on here.'

I got home in the early hours of the morning, thinking, 'Oh, God!' I just didn't know how to deal with it.

How do you discuss something like terminal cancer with your mum? I asked whether she was scared, and she said simply, 'How can I not be scared? I've never died before.'

Well, you can't argue with that. And it broke the ice. We could talk about it, openly and honestly, and work out what we were going to do. We sat down, holding hands. I wanted every piece of medical information, every fact, every opinion, every diagnosis, every test result. I was on a mission. The centre of my world changed. People always judge me on my looks and think I must spend all my time in sleazy dives. But I never have done. I was in Foyle's bookstore on Charing Cross Road in London. I practically lived in the medical section, rifling through all the books on cancer I could find, and spending a fortune, cramming facts and opinions and theories and evidence like I was doing a university degree.

At 74, my mother was too old for chemotherapy. The hospital staff were so kind, so good, but they had a sense that this was her time to go. I didn't agree, and nor did she.

She never went home to Port Sunlight – I wouldn't let her. I introduced her to organic foods, organically farmed produce, meat – lots of wholesome stuff like that. I just immersed myself in alternative therapies. We were helped by Gary Trainer, the acupuncturist – I met him at PWL, Pete Waterman's studio, when he was fixing a builder's back with needles. We didn't know what acupuncture was then, but he's since gone on to do Tina Turner and Cher.

We also sought advice from Matthew Manning, the psychic and healer, and Kay Kiernan, who practises pulsed electro-magnetic therapy. This was used to treat Russian athletes when they tore ligaments, because it was proven irrefutably that the magnetic waves regenerated muscles and vascularisation.

When Mum died, we had a coroner's report which stated that the cancer had stayed completely localised in the lung when it had been predicted to go into the breast and the brain.

I also sourced organic aloe vera juice flown in from Mexico, because it was not commonly used then; Dr Linus Pauling's vitamin C therapy; royal jelly brought in from live hives so it had literally still got the stings in; procaine Gerovital H3, which is a kind of longevity agent from Romania, invented by a doctor called Anna Aslan, and very expensive... and so the list goes on. I worked all day every day to get hold of the best available products for my mum, anything that might ease her condition, and it was the best thing I've ever done.

It was like a refrain, a coda of life for her. But she was ahead of her time, and she continued to move ahead of her time with her attitudes. In 1977, for example, she broke down crying when she saw me in my punk clothes and Lynne in her rubber skirt. 'How can I live in this rotting carcass?' she said. 'I wish I could be like that. That's what I want to be. I can't run as fast. I can't wear my heels as high.' She was grief-stricken.

So she was trapped in a rotting cage – she said that. She couldn't bear to look at her body when she bathed – she had to do it in the dark. I had to bathe her when she was ill. People ask me, wasn't that kind of strange? But how could I be repulsed by the body of somebody I'd lived inside? I bathed her like a baby, and that was a very good thing to do. She'd be very upset – 'Don't look at me! Don't look at my sagging breasts!' and things like that.

'Don't be so silly,' I'd reply gently. 'You cleaned the shit off my arse when I was wearing a nappy!' And I meant it.

There's not really any sadness attached to my feelings about those times. There's a poignancy, and a great feeling that it was absolutely the right thing to do.

Throughout those ten months I was nursing my mother, it became an increasingly expensive business. The Madonna tour came in but I couldn't do it because I was nursing my mum, and still the airplay was halted. So I

Dressing up already. Behind me is the wigwam in which I spent so much time as a child.

Inset: In a Euston photobooth! Me, Lynne and, at the bottom of the pic, Jill, on 8 April, 1982

Right: Playing at Montreux in 1985.

Left: A live show with Dead Or Alive in the '80s.

Dead or Alive - Rehearsal and Tour Itinerary as at 17/5/85

W/B 20th May
    Tim and Mike programming at Tim's home
    Steve programming at 8, Princes Street, Bootle

                                        Tony

W/B 27th May
    Tim, Mike and Steve - Rehearsal at 8, Princes Street

    28th - 31st
    Arrangement rehearsal with Mae McKenna at:-
    Studio II 313, Rehearsal, 313 Holloway Road, London, N6
    from 12 - 6pm

        Lorenza Johnson
        Jackie Challenon
        Winston Pitt   *Singers*   *P.J.*
        Cleveland Watkiss   *Ange.*
        Roy Hamilton   *Frank.*

W/B 3rd June
    Tim, Mike, Steve and Chris Payne - Rehearsal at 8, Princes St

K/B. Ban   *Bass   Drums   K/Boards.*

W/B 10th June
    Full band, Russell Bell and Backing Vocal
    Rehearsal at 8, Princes Street

                guitars. —————

Mon 17th ⚓ Load of Sound and Light (hold for band rehearsals if
                                           required)

Tue 18th   Production Rig in Liverpool - Royal Court
               (hold for band rehearsals or travel day for band to
               Liverpool)

Wed 19th   Full scale rehearsal at Royal Court
Thu 20th   "   "   "   "   "   "
Fri 21st   "   "   "   "   "   "
Sat 22nd   Travel to Edinburgh
Sun 23rd   Edinburgh Playhouse
Mon 24th   Newcastle City Hall
Tue 25th   Travel to Liverpool
Wed 26th   Liverpool Royal Court
Thu 27th   Travel to Manchester
Fri 28th   Manchester Apollo
Sat 29th   Nottingham Royal Centre
Sun 30th   Travel to Birmingham
JULY
Mon 1st   Birmingham Odeon
Tue 2nd   Bristol Hippodrome
Wed 3rd   Travel to Brighton
Thu 4th   Day off
Fri 5th   Brighton The Dome
Sat 6th   Hammersmith Odeon
Sun 7th   "   "
Mon 8th   Unloading of equipment

A page in the life of Dead Or Alive in 1985,
with a pic of me from that tour.

A selection of performances in San Francisco and, *inset*, a San Francisco ad from 1987.

A fan's eye view from all over the
world – one from Live at the Planet 1997
in Adelaide (*top left*) and the others
from G.A.Y. in London.

Top: With fan
Judy Hyde.

Middle: On a UK
club tour.

Bottom: At the
Dominion Theatre.

Top: Dead Or Alive in 1991.

Bottom: At the 2003 Mardi Gras in Hyde Park.

With Elton John at a photography exhibition in 2002.

basically had to go away and do a desperate tour of America during the last three to four weeks of Mother's life in order to pay for her treatment. I wasn't getting high fees because it was the British invasion and I wasn't considered big in Britain any more. So I was slogging around America, sometimes two shows a day, getting the money, then sending it home to get her through treatment.

I think I was away for maybe 12 days. I was in New York – it was the last gig for *Spin* magazine, a big show with dancers, the whole thing – and I was in the Essex House Hotel, along with the remnants of the management company who'd left the organisation and come with me. We'd been up all night, because it was New York – we hadn't been anywhere raving – and I got a call at seven in the morning. And, when Lynne picked up, I was told that my mum had passed away.

My dad hadn't called me because she'd slept 36 hours and she was getting some pain. I must add she'd had no morphine through the whole thing – she'd had soluble aspirin. Gary Trainer, the acupuncturist, was responsible for her pain management. She'd become tired 36 hours before and she was a bit disorientated, my dad said, and she'd told him, 'I just want to go into hospital.' And she added, 'I'm never going to come out.' So she went into hospital and they sedated her, and she went to sleep and passed in 24 hours. She died with her make-up on... and she looked fabulous.

So, of course, everything around me suddenly became, as usual, incredibly theatrical. There are first-class flights booked, but I've got this big show... My dad said, 'Don't come home – what's the point of going to the funeral?' So I thought, 'She's dead... so let me do the show and then I'll go.' So I did, and no one knew about it. I did the show, and then *Spin* wouldn't feature me, because they'd heard about it and thought I was obviously too much of a careerist bastard to deserve coverage.

In the end, I went and stayed over Christmas week with James, one of the dancers. His family were in Ohio – his mother was a country and western singer – and it was wonderful.

My dad moved on with his life, and hooked up with his best friend's ex-wife – he'd grown up with her – and they remarried very quickly. I was so happy, because my only fear was my dad being alone. He could have lived with me, but now he had a soul mate of his own.

After my mum died, I had to sell my beautiful flat because I had no money, and I had to sell it for a fraction of its actual value because I had to sell it really, really fast.

9

huge in japan

'I got offered a lot of press and TV coverage when "That's The Way (I Like It)" was a hit. But I refused to go on telly and simper on about how long it takes me to put on my make-up or to sit in a cage being pelted with custard pies.'

Where can you go but down after a Number One? What do you want to be? Madonna? No thanks. I wanted a life. I suddenly realised all that was being taken away from me and stupidly I tried to reclaim it. I didn't appreciate the luxury. I wanted to be in London, the city I had always aspired to, but suddenly I couldn't go out in London without a blacked-out limo. I couldn't go to the launderette. I couldn't go to the supermarket and buy Lean Cuisine without Jill Pringle of the *Sun* writing I had a weight problem.

It was nothing then compared to what it is now for a celebrity, but I was a highly conspicuous celebrity who happened to like to walk. And I'd never used a stylist or a hairdresser. I'd never had someone shop for my clothes, but now I had no time to shop for things I wanted. 'Oh, we'll furnish your apartment.'

No, *I* want to do it.

'But you can't, you're in Germany for three weeks.'

You're living in hotel after hotel. You're doing the same thing in foreign countries where they think it's great if they make a stage into a record and then, on the chorus, they spin it round really fast and you fall over. 'Tell us about Stock Aitken Waterman?' Move on!

Judy Garland – what do people remember her for? 'Over the Rainbow', but there were so many other things that she did. You have this one hit and people associate you with that for ever. I accept now that I'm fortunate to have had a success like 'Spin Me' but, at times, it was very depressing. I thought, 'I'm never going to move on from that song.'

In order to function in music, you've got to be fundamentally brainless. Where are the creative people? They've all gone because they've all been driven mad by it and OD'd, and that's not going to happen to me. Obviously, you have to have an enormous amount of tenacity to function in the music industry, and to overcome the hurdles put in front of you by the corporate industry and the crap you've got to repeat to shitty magazines. What was it like to work with Stock Aitken

Waterman? It's been said a thousand times, so I've got nothing more to say on that at all.

Oh, the questions. Whenever I toured, I'd get, 'Well, how does it feel to be in Dallas?'

And you really want to say, 'I don't fucking know, because I've just got off the plane. I've been in some piss-stinking, beer-soaked nightclub waiting for the sound man to show up and now I'm at the hotel trying to trowel make-up on. I've got to be on stage 'til two in the morning and leave town at seven. I don't *know*.'

'What can we expect from the show tonight?'

'Exactly the same as the previous night, and the night before that...' because it's all repetition. There's no spontaneity in music.

The truth is, no matter how much I might need the money, I no longer want to do a world tour; I don't want to headline a stadium; I don't want to do a merchandise deal... so what's in it for me? Because a lot was in it for all of you bastards when I was up and running, so what's in it for me now? Spin-offs, like this book and a lot of TV work, which means I can actually be in one place with Michael, my partner, not hiking around the world in a high-pressure environment doing the same thing every night.

Nobody really realises that the older you are, the longer your stage show, when you're really ready for your bath and your commode. Because you've got more history, so the show's got to be longer.

And I have got a history, although the tangible

reminders of that history are not always easy to come by. I'll always remember being on *Top of the Pops* and everyone like Peter Powell and Janice Long were congratulating me on the gold discs, and I went, 'Discs? Oh, I've gone gold? Where's mine?' Everyone had one but me.

Pop music used to excite me, but I got into it and I realised it was a pile of shit. Where are the creative artists? Drugged up, drunk, because they can't get in, because they've got something to say. Look at Courtney Love – it doesn't get any better than 'Celebrity Skin'. 'Well, no, she's a loose cannon. We're not going to even listen to her. I'll tell you what – we'll put, who is it, Jessica Simpson's sister at Number One.' Give me a break!

We parted from Stock Aitken Waterman because, at the time of my mother's death, we were recording *Mad, Bad and Dangerous to Know,* and I wouldn't let them write for us. They'd written 'Respectable' for us before Mel & Kim recorded it, so they might not have had motivation to carry on recording with us because they could write for other people. Also, my fellow band members, Mike Percy and Tim Lever, needed some publishing royalties. So I had to stand firm. And I wasn't quite sure how to interpret someone else's song then. It's like trying to have children and somebody shoves you an adopted baby. I didn't know what to do with the damn thing!

I was delighted when my singles stopped making the Top 20. What was I gaining from being in the Top 20?

All I was getting was more pressure to recreate the same formula. 'Do "Spin Me" again... do "Spin Me" again...'

Every record I took in, they'd go, 'It's not exactly "Spin Me".'

So I'd go, 'Why don't you fucking put "Spin Me" out again?'

And guess what, they did! It's been reissued more times than I can count. But it gets me in the door, I suppose – it's like a forged ID to be allowed to drink alcohol when you're under age.

Some of the doors that opened for us became opportunities to do and see things that we'd never have had a chance to do otherwise. Like touring Japan, where success came really easily.

Two weeks of intensive work, being pampered like King Faroukh, luxury and gifts, electronic gadgets, the presidential suite at the Hilton Hotel. Hot and cold running Rolls-Royces, motorcades to get me everywhere and, guess what, I didn't speak the language. How great was that?

I think when the Japanese took to me in such a big way it was very much the Kabuki theatre thing and their acceptance of androgyny, and an undercurrent of homosexuality that's suppressed in their culture. I mean, they're kinky, the Japanese. They have all those love hotels and sex toys and rubberwear, but it's all very hidden. But, to them, I was really out there, but I wasn't Japanese, so they could show me off, love me and then ship me back home. I was a bit of a peep show for them and I look like a cartoon.

They were great and they work like slaves, but they work you like a slave, too. But anything you do, they do. If you're working 'til 5.00am, they're there. They'll sleep on their feet. I function that way – whatever needs doing, I'll keep on going and I won't turn off until I've completed my contractual obligations. I'm really not difficult to work with. I will do what I'm contractually obliged to do and sometimes more, but the more is *my* option.

There was constant adulation and attention in Japan, too, but they're very polite about it and I can't understand what they're saying. It's only two weeks out of your life every couple of years, and you don't have to be there all the time, so it's great. And, when your job's finished, they more or less walk past you in the street, but that's great. That's showbiz; I understand that.

The Japanese paid very, very well indeed. It was rumoured quite strongly that I own Japanese brothels and that's where all my finance came from. I was asked this quite seriously at the time of *Evolution* by a journalist – it was everywhere that I ran Japanese brothels. God, I wish I did! Sling me a kimono – I'll be there! Of course, there have been rumours, but I wrote my own songs and I had a very lucrative Performing Rights Society royalty system, plus publishing royalties four times a year – it was enough for me.

Nude, produced in 1986, was about the sense of loss – 'Give It Back', 'Our Love Is Mine', 'Baby, Don't Say Goodbye', 'I Cannot Carry On'... I didn't know that when it was coming out. It was about six years later that I realised that. It contained a lot of hurt and anger. We've all lost things but the first real loss, the biggest thing that I'd lost to that date, was Mum. I hadn't just lost her physical presence – I'd lost a battle against cancer, because I took that on as though I had cancer myself.

It consumed every second of my existence – trawling bookshops, medical suppliers, reading everything. We didn't have the Internet then, so it was all read, read, read and phone calls and, oh, God, it was such a learning curve and so fast. I learned I had to separate the good from the bad, make a choice, and I was making that choice as 'if it was me, what would I choose?' She was in shock, so I had to make all the choices, and it was 22 hours a day, seven days a week. When she died, I sort of exhaled – 'The battle's over. I've lost.'

I'd have fought that for five years, for ten years, for any amount of time. And it opened up a lot of other avenues for me, in helping my understanding of other medical matters. Medicine is necessary, but we treat the symptom and not the cause. We need to treat the cause and, by the time the symptom has emerged, the cause is too far buried beneath the symptom. We suppress but we do things that are so self-destructive and there are so many causes. I am at a point at which I think if you're going to get cancer, you're going to get it anyway. It's nothing to do with smoking – it's the worrying about smoking and the guilt. It's fear, fear, fear. 'Don't eat this – it clogs your arteries... Oh, God, I really like it, but I shouldn't be eating it – I wish I could stop.' It's like you're programmed to self-destruct.

Nude was a battle, too. I wasn't nude on the cover – I had knickers on, but it upset people. They wouldn't print the cover in the factory after the first run, and they kept the inner sleeve out because I was wearing a John Richmond T-shirt with a penis on it. Then the reps wouldn't carry it in their cars around the shops – they used to take the stock round in boxes. I wasn't nude – but they were shocked.

I don't know what I was trying to do then, but it seemed really odd in hindsight that Prince was allowed to do it, sitting in a lily looking like a midget, but me, even though I looked nice, I wasn't allowed to do it. So then it was like, 'Either we change the covers or we're gonna pull the album.'

'I'm not going to change the cover – pull it.' I was adamant.

So they pulled the album, but it went on to huge success in Japan.

Also, we produced it ourselves. We'd never done that before, so that was great. I mean, I find faults now in the production when I listen to tracks like 'Give It Back' and 'That Love Is Mine'. And there are a couple of other tracks where I was just experimenting – like 'I Don't Wanna Be Your Boyfriend' which is like a Philly sound. It was 'Let's try this... let's have a go at that...'

That incarnation of Dead or Alive was a great team – Mike Lever, Tim Percy and Steve Coy, and Tracy

Ackerman and Laura Pallas as backing singers. But it's not so much about production – it's about editing and shortening things. Because it was so good, we'd just gone on and everything was overlong. It was great, that album, really good. OK, the sounds are dated now but then a song's a song, and songs don't date. Tracks like 'Give It Back' and 'That Love Is Mine' were far superior to 'Spin Me Round', and so is 'Baby Don't Say Goodbye' and 'I Don't Wanna Be Your Boyfriend'. It was a body of work, not the production.

After *Nude*, we left Epic. We then started to record our own records ourselves and license them to various record companies around the world. We simply went back to operating like an indie band but the sales were considerably bigger because of the previous big success. And because the albums sold well, especially in Japan, they all built up a very nice living for me.

It sold so well in Japan I didn't need to go anywhere. I had my house, and I helped a lot of my friends who were in trouble with unfortunate diseases and their finance problems. I got involved in things that I really wanted to do. I wasn't that aware of what AIDS was at that time, but somebody I knew came down with AIDS and it was very serious. When he was in hospital after seizures, I went to the hospital and I was mortified to see young people in there in that condition, and I got very involved there.

Eventually, I got banned from the hospital, because there were young boys in there whose throats and chests were ulcerated – they couldn't swallow due to the drugs they'd had. I still had some aloe vera that I'd had flown in from Mexico for my mother, so I was buying it by the crateload, taking them undiluted aloe vera and just saying, 'Drink this.' All the ulcers and sores and radiation burns went in the throat. And what do you know? I was called to a room and told, 'Don't come back any more.' They couldn't break the regulations for someone who wasn't qualified, which meant I wasn't able to go on with what I was doing.

Funnily enough, the same thing happened when I tried to donate money to the facial reconstruction charity called Face the World. It was at the time of *Big Brother*, but they weren't able to accept my money because I couldn't tell them what I was doing – *Big Brother* is very strict about you not letting anyone know you're going in, but understandably charities need to know where their money is coming from. Face the World might still get my cheque. Martin Kelly now runs the charity, and it was because of him that I felt drawn to the charity. Unbelievably, he was an extra, one of the models, in my video 'Save You All My Kisses'. He went on to become a major reconstructive surgeon, and he visits Developing World countries and offers reconstructive surgery to kids in desperate need. He did an interview in *Tatler* and I just thought, 'This sounds so great – this is where I want my share of the charity money to go.' I just wanted to know some details so I could go and speak eloquently and visit the kids and be there when they're doing the operations.

But at that point we couldn't mention the *Big Brother*

thing, because the whole point was not to tell anyone, because before you know it it's in the papers and then they wouldn't have had me on the show. And we dealt with so much shit I ended up on tranquillisers, because I had to give the *Big Brother* people his name. They wouldn't send us anything via the Internet.

Michael sent them letters, he did everything. He sat on the computer and the phone – someone else's phone, we couldn't afford to pay at the time – making national and international calls to hospitals all over the place. It had touched my heart, the work that the charity was doing, but it was so frustrating not being able to donate money because of the red tape.

10

the naughty nineties

'One kids' television show refused to play my record because they said I looked too weird in the video. In the end, they put on a Marilyn Manson video. How ridiculous is that?'

Oh, God, the Nineties. I think I lost the Nineties. I'm not really good on the years – life's just one long year – but I suppose the decade started for me with *Fan the Flame*, which was different from what we'd done before. I had a project to write seven songs every Sunday and I was working with the wonderful Peter Oxendale. He's a musicologist and he knows exactly how people write. You take a bridge off an Andrews Sisters song, and you take a verse off a Billie Holiday song, and you take a chorus off a pop song, and you reverse it all round, so that the chorus becomes the verse, so you've got them hooked. It's all a jigsaw process. He could transpose all the things together and change the relevant note in a much more intelligent way than, for instance, Madonna does.

Anyway, Peter Oxendale helped me through that. Any challenge he threw at me, I ran with, and the vocals were a process of writing. They were all done on a cassette in the house on a Sunday, and if we got seven done we were laughing. Then, after seven, we'd go in the studio on the Tuesday and choose what we would do, but it was a lot of creative wank, and there was a lot of drinking going on in the band at that time. I can't work in that atmosphere, so I was at the gym a lot. I got to do guide vocals, and the guide vocals were a process of writing.

Then, before you knew it, the pressure was on to go to Japan. I needed to get to Japan really quick with *Fan the Flame*. The next thing I heard, 'Total Stranger' was going to be covered by Barbra Streisand. There were meetings set up and everything, and then it was pulled; I don't know why. Somebody called me up and said, 'Ms Streisand...' and I said, 'She'll always be Babs to me...' I really wanted to write for Barbra – or with her. I just thought it would be a hoot because she's just an old Jewish *yentl*, isn't she? I've always loved Barbra Streisand – she was my idea of beauty in the 1960s.

People ask me why I decided to go from dance music to *Fan the Flame*. But, you know, there is no such thing as 'dance' music. There's just music and you put a beat that's danceable to it. I just thought I would like to do something different.

We did a great show for the *Fan the Flame* tour – it was dance, but we had ballet dancers and video projections of roses on fire... It was sound and vision, but someone decided that I wasn't suitable material to turn into Frank Sinatra and it just kind of sabotaged that album.

But I'm glad, because I rewrote 'Total Stranger' into a track called 'I'm a Star' for the *Nukleopatra* album which was much more what I felt. I thought that was great – an ad-lib over the backing track. The track 'Nukleopatra' was about reincarnation, because it was a combination of 'nuclear' (bomb) and 'patra' which is kind of slang for Peter. Nukleopatra – that's me. But I love the words – '*I saw an advertisement in a magazine, so I came to see you to find out who I'd been, you said I was queen...*' It's got great lyrics – '*King of the she-male race...*'

I thought the Egyptian times were very futuristic – the miniskirt, the eyeliner, the wigs, the adornments of the Egyptians, all of that was very much what the youth-quake was about in the 1960s here. I believe that they could travel, I believe they could fly and I believe they probably had the equivalent of motorbikes and, even now, beauty products find their roots in Ancient Egypt. Glycolic acids are from milk, and people use lactic acids now in skin care – the Egyptians were doing exactly that. Sun block, kohl on the eyes – all of them were from Egypt. The Egyptians knew a thing or two about a thing or two.

We also did a Blondie cover for that album. I wanted to

do 'Dreaming', but 'Picture This' was everyone else's choice for some reason. I'd like to have done 'Atomic' or 'Looking on the Bright Side' or 'I Can See Clearly Now', which is a good solo track; there was a world of possibilities from the Blondie catalogue... Oh, God, she blows me away. She's a poet. And her life story in that book, *Making Tracks*... She was too pretty and no one would take her seriously and then, at the ripe old age of 34 or 35, 'Denis Denis' exploded.

I met her and she was adorable, a real street girl. I know that she's like Bardot – she was a hostage to her own beauty. She was born that way and she's always going to be living in the shadow of her image at its peak, 'Heart of Glass'. When she's on TV now, they show 'Heart of Glass' and then she's sitting there with rollers in or something, because that's the way she is. I saw her on some programme a few years ago – she had rollers in for the sound check and no one really gets it. It's a uniquely New York sensibility that she's got.

And that lyric – '*When I met you in the restaurant, you could tell I was no debutante...*' and '*People stop and stare at me, I don't want to live on charity, Is it real or is it make believe? People stop and stare at me, We just walk on by just to have our dream...*' It's a song of hope and moving on, and I became obsessed with that. And then I met Michael in a restaurant... but I wasn't a debutante!

It was just an event, that album, a real event. Fabulous! I loved it, really loved it, particularly the track 'Nukleopatra'.

In 1994, I did the Glam single 'Sex Drive', then, in 1995, I did the 'Rebel Rebel' single under the name of International Chrysis. Why International Chrysis? She was an influence. Chrysis was a transsexual, leader of the trans group called Hot Peaches, a big force in fashion and drag shows. She was also in a big Hollywood movie – she played José Malpica in Sidney Lumet's *Q&A* – in which she is dead in the last scene, and she died of cancer on the day of the première in 1990. Priscilla Presley was modelled on Chrysis – Elvis had met her, apparently. Chrysis's look was like a Bobbie Gentry wig, the five pairs of eyelashes, the polo-neck leotard with a hand-cut belt and thick black tights. There were photos of Chrysis in a book called *The Queens* that's pretty hard to get now.

Many years later, I got to work with a girl who's featured in Madonna's book *Sex*. She's in the comic at the back, under the name of Chiclet. I didn't know this, but she – her name was Gina – did a lot of choreography for Madonna and put that book together with Steven Meisel. Gina choreographed the *Erotica* thing for Madonna and then, when I met her, she was a model for Thierry Mugler. Beautiful girl, looked like Bardot at her peak – a really, really beautiful girl, very full figured. Anyway, she came to England to choreograph some shows for me.

She eventually got to my house and she had this beautiful lace gown that she split up the front and used to wear white knickers underneath and thigh-high boots and go for walks at night.

She did a lot of choreography and putting videos together – like the 'Rebel Rebel' video. Gina lived with me for two to three years, and she was an event.

I've got an open door for, you know, waifs and strays. But that stray has got to bring something attached to its tail, and Gina was very responsible for me learning to go from the big stage to small ones and do incredible American tours that were so disorganised. You know, the stages weren't right and we couldn't do laundry. But she taught me things like, if you're good, you can do it on a beer mat and the audience can't smell you and nobody can smell a photograph, so don't be crying about your laundry.

The gigs were just such an event because I was working with dancers from the Alvin Ailey troupe. We did these shows in America where the black guys were painted blacker – we painted them absolute jet-black – and I came out of a trunk covered in various flags but ultimately emerged in a swastika sari painted gold. Then Gina would slide round a pole in a cartwheel and do the whole performance on a handstand and such like. But then the whole American music industry thought I was a fascist because I was wearing a swastika sari and the gigs were getting pulled and I ended up setting fire to a flag in Texas and the building rioted.

I had been told that I could do anything I wanted. 'Anything? *Anything?*'

'Absolutely anything,' they said.

'Take a shit on the floor?'

'Yeah.'

'Set fire to something?'

'Yeah.'

So I set fire to an American flag in Texas and, from then on, I was escorted on stage by up to 30 policemen. So we turned it into part of the show; they carried me on in handcuffs. It's all over the Internet that tour. It was just one of those in the 1990s without the band – I just wanted to do it with a dance troupe, because of the rigidity of working with musicians.

Then it wasn't considered such a crime to burn the American flag. But also, when we burned that one, we climbed up a pole at the hotel in Texas and took all the flags and I was making saris out of them – they were being sewn together with swastikas and the gay flag. The swastika is an Indian symbol but people weren't getting it. I don't agree with burying symbols of fear from history, because it gives it power. Put it everywhere!

On another of these tours, I had a complete breakdown on the streets of America. I was in New York with the team of dancers and one of them didn't tell me he had AIDS. There were homeless people in the doorways and it was just awful – I was just taking the gig fees and giving it away in the street. I'm not Mother Teresa but I couldn't give it to a charity – it was like, what about the people on the street? And then I was told I couldn't do it because of the IRS – the tax system in America. You get taxed when you earn and I was just getting the gig fee.

There's an album out there called *Fan the Flame Pt II* which I recorded in Texas. I said, 'Get me a piano player and get me some sheet music,' and they did. And the piano player was horrified by how I looked. So it was just segments and I said, 'I've got to scrap this.' We'd designed the cover and were just gonna scrap it, and whaddya know? I left it and somebody took the master tape and released it, selling it on the Internet with my sleeve notes, everything! It's scraps of out-of-tune songs, it's a mess, it's shit. I wanted to do good covers of 'Will You Still Love Me Tomorrow?' and 'I Wish You Love' and 'Is That All There Is?' – all these great songs together, just acoustically. How can I finish it? Someone took the master tapes from the studio. It should be left to rot, that album, because it wasn't an album. And I resent the vultures, the shits, the imbeciles, the fans who continue to buy it for hundreds of dollars because they're stealing, too. What I intended to do was sell it on the merchandise stall and take the profits every night and drive round in the car to the homeless people with AIDS and give it to them in cash.

After we left Epic, Avex came on board and wanted us to re-record all of our back catalogue. We said no. They said, 'Give us six new songs and six old ones,' and that was *Fragile*. We had 12 days to do it in and no new songs. The best track on that is called 'Isn't It a Pity' – that's the work I'm proudest of on that album. That was written on my birthday, a very miserable birthday, and it was done in less than two hours from start to finish. Completely done, there you go. That's how quick I work.

We also did three cover versions for tribute albums at the end of the decade – we were commissioned to do them by Cleopatra Records in Los Angeles. First, there was Madonna's 'Why Is It So Hard?' in 1999. Why did I do it if I don't like Madonna? Because I got $35,000 to do it and I needed the goddamn money! I had to do a Madonna track – it was an album compilation and I wanted to do 'Papa Don't Preach' but Martin Degville of Sigue Sigue Sputnik was doing that and I couldn't find a Madonna track that I liked. I don't even like that one – it's frightful!

The same year we did U2's 'Even Better Than the Real Thing' – well, I am! Haven't you worked out what the lyrics are about? There was a record by Garbage called 'Queer' and I remember hearing that, because I love Garbage. Shirley Manson is great – her energy is great. 'The queerest of the queer' – I think that's what 'Even Better Than the Real Thing' is about. Think about it – 'even better than the real thing'.

I love U2. Right from '11 O'clock Tick Tock', when they were a young Irish band, U2 came to Eric's. I mean, I don't have any opinion on the people in the band – I know fuck all about them – but I know that every time they put a record out it's great. Everything they do – 'Where the Streets Have No Name'– top that, bitches. U2 are fucking fantastic! What would you think I'd listen to? Whatever it is, you've got it wrong.

Then the following year we did Prince's 'Pop Life'. I wanted to do 'Why Should I Love You' which is on the Kate Bush album *The Red Shoes*, but I thought Prince had written it – it was a duet, but Kate Bush wrote it. So

I had to do 'Pop Life'. I really admire his musical output, but I wish someone would throw a bucket of water over him to wake him up, because he's one of the sons of the silent age, isn't he? Like the silent-movie stars. You know what goes on around Prince – no one can look at him. I wasn't expecting him to be gregarious and vivacious, but, when he was here for the Brit Awards, no one could look at him or have eye contact – he's either a very, very shy individual or he still thinks he's Gloria Swanson. There must be a person underneath there, but what's he trying to protect?

I've met Prince and it was a strange experience. I was in a club called The Bank in Earl's Court in London and I was with Gina and she used to perform a lot to records. She used to do ballet and she could lip-sync, and she was going off to Crystal Waters's 'Gypsy Woman' against the mirrors. So she was doing this performance in the club just on the dance floor and, suddenly, the lights went down and Prince had arrived with all of his monkeys, and they had one booth. So I said I wanted the lights up; Prince wants them down. Up... down... up... down... so I went to the DJ and said, 'Have you got any Prince records?'

'Yeah, I've got them all.'

'Right – put them all on.'

So then Prince left when all of his records came on.

But what I also remember about the 1990s were some very strange encounters. During this time I was in Hollywood, and I spent a lot of time at the Sunset

Marquis Hotel while I was negotiating with Epic – they would not release 'Come Home With Me Baby'. It had been 13 weeks at Number One in the dance singles chart – it held off Michael Jackson, Janet Jackson and Prince, and it was the longest-ever Number One in the *Billboard* dance chart – but they didn't deem it suitable for release, fundamentally because the video was full of religious imagery. And I was in a choreographed routine with seven male dancers, one of whom was wearing a T-shirt with 'God' written on it while I was singing *'Come home with me'*. That video was really not right for America, according to them.

But, shortly before I left for LA, I was in the Atlantic bar in Glasshouse Street in London and I was approached by a group of American people who kept sending champagne over to me. I was hanging out with an Australian girl who worked in the cloakroom, reading the magazines, and somebody wanted to meet me. It turned out to be David Duchovny from *The X-Files*. Nothing at all sexual happened but I went for dinner with him in a restaurant called Sarastros in Covent Garden, and met David Soul, David Ginola and various other people. I wasn't aware of who they were, because I didn't watch football and I didn't watch *The X-Files* – but a small, luxurious house in the lower hills of Hollywood was made available, where I could go and stay whenever I wanted. I had keys, so I used to go and stay there a lot.

In the early 1990s, I was booked to play the Limelight in New York. Gina put together the Alvin Ailey Dance

Troop for me, and we arrived at the Limelight, where Michael Alig, who was running the Limelight, answered the door with three pigs' noses on and a curly wig. First of all, he wouldn't let me in because he didn't recognise me, and then we discovered he'd built a stage of hanging bodies – dead or alive – and I said, 'I'm not singing with that. Take it down.'

'Who do you think you are, girl?' he said.

So I just went back to the hotel. It turned into a gangster shit – $40,000 for one gig and all the tickets sold – and there were people trying to break in, really bad people. So Gina and I went down the fire exit and went to places called Sally's Hideaway and Edelweiss, which are well-known tranny bars but full of Hollywood actors, and a lot of people knew Gina. At the time, she was wearing a corset that Mr Pearl had made – it was an incredible iridescently jewelled butterfly – and somebody approached us. Gina knew them and she said, 'Listen, we've got to go to Long Island...' and the next thing I knew we were being driven with a load of bodyguards to Eddie Murphy's house.

He had a house with thick glass walls, with tropical fish and miniature sharks – the usual film star splendour thing. His bath was nearly as big as a room, and was made of thick glass, inside which were eels and luminescent fish swimming around, so, when you had a bath, you were in the ocean. When you go in those people's houses, it's beyond fantasy... you can't conceive what they have.

Did he know who I was? Well, at the time, I was

wearing bubblegum-pink rubber catsuits with vintage Vivienne Westwood Sex boots, and I had this filthy, dark brown/blonde kind of tiger hair that I bleached with Domestos, inspired by Debbie Harry but one step further. And I was wearing incredible amounts of deliberately grotesque make-up – like a white face with Liza Minnelli *Cabaret*-blue eye-shadow, and I had white nail extensions. So it was very extreme and, well, everybody seemed to know who I was.

After that, we moved into a suite at Essex House, which was a very, very famous hotel where Jean Harlow used to stay – David Letterman lives there now. And we had a triplex, three-bedroom suite and 24-hour car service, two bodyguards and open charge accounts at Bergdorf Goodman's and all the department stores in New York. You haven't lived 'til you've got your suite at Essex House with open charge accounts at the most exclusive department stores, who look at you like you're crazy when you walk in, and you can say, 'Give me those six Chanel bags,' and shop for $60,000 worth of goods and dump them all into the car and then give them away as presents or sell them for cash. That sort of standard of living has to be seen to be believed! So, naturally, we blew the rest of the tour!

11
plastic fantastic

'If you own a car, you change that every few years, and that's just what I'm doing with my appearance.'

I've always played with make-up. As young child, I used paint – kids' paints – all over my face, all over my body, all over the walls, because there wasn't enough paper to paint what I wanted to paint. I just *needed* to paint everywhere.

Then I thought I'd like to sculpt. So I had plasticine and clay, and I made jewellery out of macaroni and dipped it in food colouring when I ran out of paint. I just made things all the time. I'd make my own moulds out of plasticine and such like, and put things inside. I'd Spirograph all over the ceiling. I should have been institutionalised then!

My mother was quite happy about it all, and my dad had the good grace just to think it was creative expression. He didn't say anything, because he had what he needed – his *Sunday Times*, his wife, his job.

Children shouldn't be stunted in their growth. Don't say to a kid, 'Don't write on the wall!' Why not? You can paint over it. You keep the child's first school painting, so why shouldn't the kid write on the wall? It's not as if I was writing 'shit' and 'piss' or 'Liverpool FC'. I was making pretty pictures and learning.

When my mother went through her early-morning ritual, it wasn't just the make-up – she prepared for the world. It was a meditative thing and she did her hair and took a long bath and she was prepared for anything. It's very much the pattern that I've come to follow in later life. Make-up sounds like a falsification, but you must realise the importance of make-up. If it wasn't for Max Factor, we'd never have had the big movie stars, would we? That is what made them gods and goddesses. Make-up was very important in society, and in our aspirations and our dreams, and, if the big movie stars of the day – the Dietrichs, the Garbos, the Clarke Gables, the Montgomery Clifts, the Liz Taylors – were seen without make-up, we'd have had nothing to look up to. Make-up made people hold their heads up, and it also gives them a positive attitude. Make-up sounds like it's false. It's not – it's volume up, contrast up, just to emphasise what is there.

We appreciate art in galleries – Renoirs, Picassos –

because it's on a non-living, non-moving piece of material. But it's still make-up – paint is still make-up. And we paint ourselves but, instead of being hung in some boring gallery, we're walking round the streets all day every day, feeling better about ourselves. It should be mandatory – everyone should wear make-up! If I get into government, people are going to get a make-up allowance and they're going to have to wear it, because it might let them express something that's already in there.

It's more functional than deodorant, isn't it? I'd rather somebody smelled bad and looked good, than looked bad and smelled great. That's why we should love with our hearts. We should all be blind, then we would love with our hearts and not our eyes – and we do love with our eyes. I don't give a shit what people say about liking the 'inside'– we can't mind-read. You can't tell what someone's like inside – it takes time and we have no time. Society is moving quicker and there's more of everything – too much television, too many magazines, too many clubs. We're all rushing, chasing our tails, so we've got no time to get to know each other. So how we look is our membership card to society and acceptance, and people will come inside and find all the wonder that's in you and love you, too.

But how many shops do you see with bricked-up fronts? No one's going to go in. We are our own shop window for what's inside. We display all of our jewels and, frankly, all of my jewels are for display. I enjoy them. And they're all for sale.

I've always been a supporter of plastic surgery, even when it was a dirty word. And look at it now! It was a need in me to become what I became, because I was that before and I didn't recognise myself any more. I've had many lives, I know it. But I'm still in the process of understanding it all. For example, my vast medical knowledge... where does it come from? My way with words that rhyme... where does that come from? I've never written a thing down. You can ask Stock Aitken Waterman that – it's out, first take. My recovery capacity, my energy force, my intuition... I know that I've been here before, several times, and this is the last time. I don't want to come back, because I haven't learned a damn thing and society hasn't progressed. Well, maybe it has, but it's all been downhill. My former lives were very difficult for me and, for some deluded reason, I must have thought, 'Oh great! It's 1959 and it'll be the age of Aquarius, harmony and understanding...' so I came merrily whooshing down the birth canal, and then I saw what the world was like. I was, 'Oh, God, let me get back up there again...'

It wasn't as if I wanted to transform myself into a particular look. I wasn't putting anything there that wasn't there – I was just chipping away the clay. The tattoos were already there. I just removed the film, the membrane of skin that had formed over them. It was a process of stripping naked. It was like I had a mask on.

The Red Indian picture when I was a child – it was only after a great deal of persuasion that I removed that Red

Indian mask that was on the top of the tent. I wore that all the time, mainly because it had a nice black plait attached to it, but I liked the face as a child. Westerns traumatised me. I never ever saw the cowboy as the hero – I was obsessed with the native American Indian culture.

That outfit was worn seven days a week. I had set things that could not be removed and I was allowed the luxury of being able to do that. There is a reason why a child locks on to things like that, or why some children just get up and play the piano effortlessly. We're all born again. We've all been here before – there is no death.

So why was it important for me to chip away at that clay? Because it had to be me! I think I was great-looking before, but it wasn't... well... *me*. I think Barbra Streisand is great-looking, but I'd kind of get a shock if I woke up and saw her face looking back at me in the mirror. I think Whoopi Goldberg's great-looking, but if I woke up one morning and saw her in the mirror, with my mind and my eyes looking out of it, I'd be traumatised, because it wouldn't be me. You know you try on an outfit and you can go, 'It's really nice... but it's not me'? I was like that with my own face.

I didn't have a specific idea of what I wanted to look like – I already looked like that. I just digitally enhanced myself, the way photos are done, except that my digital enhancing was done with a scalpel and mallet and a syringe. Then again, everyone – from the minute they wake up – is doing a self-transformation, but where are the boundaries of acceptability? A man wakes up every morning... he shaves... doesn't he want everyone to see his beard? Most men shave. Women bleach their hair and describe themselves as blonde. Men put on trousers, underwear, socks – that's all a process of transformation but it's temporary. The beard grows back by five o'clock. So you wait and then you take it off the next day.

Everyone is tweaking. Since we've become 'civilised', we've tweaked more. Tribal rituals are more physical tweaking – scarring, piercings, paintings, the discs in the lips, the neck rings. Then it became 'OK, we won't do that – that's a bit self-mutilation... So what we'll do is put on a pin-stripe suit, sensible shoes and some grey socks – but underneath we've got suspenders.'

Everyone is modifying to some degree. I don't believe in the fountain of youth. You can't buy the fountain of youth in Selfridges. Cream – hope in a jar – that, to me, is absolute hypocrisy and a waste of money. The only way to fix it is to cut it off. People who are ageing naturally often say, 'I'm so wrinkly and I'm so old, so I'm going to buy myself a nice new car...' – you're no better off. How horrifying – a nice, shiny new car with an old face looking out the side window! It's much better to have a new face looking out of a rusty old car. 'Oh, I can't do this to myself – I could have a nice three-week holiday in Mexico for that.' You know what? A new face looks a damn sight better than a Mexican blanket and it lasts longer.

It's just different priorities. You live in your body, you live in your house. Does anybody move into a house and think, 'Oh, this is exactly as I wanted it to be, with that mock flock wallpaper and the brown nylon carpet and the yellow sofa...'? No – they end up saying, 'I'm going to alter this, alter that...' Nobody berates them for it or finds it questionable. And you know what? Your house can burn down!

I live in this body. Underneath this skin and this bone and this blood is a soul, and underneath that soul is something that's higher than a spirit. It's looking out and it has to live in the right circumstances and surroundings, the right tent. This is just the chassis or the body of a car for the engine inside me, and it had to be right. You don't put a Ferrari engine in a Ford Cortina.

My surgery was so far removed from vanity – it was sanity. If you – assuming you're white – woke up tomorrow and you were black, how would you feel? And I don't mean in a racist way – the same is true if you're black and you woke up white. If you did wake up and you had some kind of skin condition that wouldn't kill you, but you're suddenly black – or vice versa – how would you feel? It wouldn't be right for you, would it? If you're a bloke, and you woke up tomorrow with two huge breasts that had grown overnight, how would you feel? You could cover them with a jumper and no one would know and they might be very nice breasts, but how would you feel?

You really want to say, 'I'd be fine about it, because I'm OK inside.' But you wouldn't be. You might be really nice-looking – black... white... with breasts... without – but how would you feel? Forget political correctness – how would you *feel*? You'd just think, 'This isn't me.'

So, when I got to the age of about three or four, where I could start to make choices, I knew it wasn't me. Yes, even at that age, as a child, I knew it wasn't me. So I used all the things that adults use, like adornments, perfectly acceptable things in adult society: a Red Indian headdress, a fringe squaw dress and a ukulele. But that wasn't enough, they were only temporary; they came off. I wanted something that didn't come off, because it's me.

I didn't want a prosthetic limb which is make-up and clever photography. I didn't want a screw-on leg that looks the same and walks the same but it isn't quite the same and comes off at night. I wanted the real thing, so I made myself into the real thing, the real me. But I didn't *want* it – I had to have it! What do you do if you've got a kidney stone? You have to get it blasted. I didn't want it – I *needed* it.

My first nose job cost me about £850 – anybody could have afforded it. It was done by Dr Gipson and that included two nights in a convent in Sefton Park. Yes, nuns were running the hospital!

Some people ask if I had a complete picture in mind after I'd had that done. I didn't, no. It was like when I painted the *Big Brother* picture – I didn't know what I was going to do. I just went with the paints. The pole in the tent – the nose is the pole that holds up the tent and I needed to start from a centre point and work outwards. Not as much has been done as people might think; minor changes can make a huge difference. Lips, nose, cheeks...

no eyes, and no brow lift at all – and I can get an affidavit off the surgeon to prove it.

I read a report in a paper in which a doctor claimed I'd had £50,000 of surgery, and it was so funny because, some years ago, I actually went to see that doctor, and I said to him that I wanted something done with my nose. He referred me to a hospital for gender reassignment, and he said, 'I think you'd be happier with a vagina plasticy.'

So I said, 'Well, *you're* a cunt!' and walked out. That was the last I saw of him and, lo and behold, he ends up in the papers making up stories about what I've had done.

People ask whether it ever occurred to me that it could all go wrong. But, when people go for a haircut, do they sit there and go, 'Oh, God, what if this goes wrong?' You might say that your hair will grow back again, but your nose or cheeks would be permanently damaged. But you can get them built back. That happens to boxers and people in car accidents all the time. They take a little piece out of your ear and put that in and it's back. There's nothing they can do that they can't undo – except for the injectables, which mesh with the tissue and are highly dangerous.

I didn't do any research before I started. You have to start somewhere and I thought I'd be proactive – I'd start that way and then I'd research. Of course, I've researched plenty now that I've been through it all. But my research now in the interests of other people is vast, and I'm finding out more and more. I'm meeting some really good people who I'm going along to see to be aware of the reconstructive side of things, and to find out what can be done for people. I really want to get involved in that because I know what it's like to be mutilated and disfigured, and how cruel people can be when they see you on the street. Imagine a child going through that – it's awful for them. What a start in life that is.

It's no easier for an adult, but maybe they've learned resignation; they're resigned to the fact that there's no light at the end of the tunnel, but there can be. There *is* light at the end of the tunnel and, in this day and age – when they can reattach limbs, fingers, genitalia... you name it – fixing a nose that's been eaten away by cancer is well within modern capability. The same goes for a breast that has to be removed, or a face with nerve damage, they can all be made to look OK. So much can be done, but people don't know where to go. Practitioners in this field tend not to court publicity – you have to find them, because when you've found them it means you're serious. But people don't know where to look, because there's so much white noise out there.

People think I've been lifted, stretched, plucked and tucked more times than a Holiday Inn bedsheet, but that's bollocks. I am not in denial about what I've done – and denial ain't a river in Egypt. So, despite what you might read elsewhere, let me be clear about what I've actually had done.

I had one nose job in 1985 and it was crooked, because I had to do *Top of the Pops* for 'You Spin Me Round' and removed the bandage after five days, so it didn't have time to set in its splint. That's when I wore the eye-patch, to cover the bruising.

Later, I had cheek implants. I visited an eminent plastic surgeon and he corrected my nose with a graft and went on to do cheek implants, but they didn't work so I had them taken out.

In 1989, I had probably the first Botox injection in the UK. I hated the fact that, once my nose had been reduced, I had a deep furrow in the brow when I sang – I called it the George Michael bum forehead, because George Michael looks like he's got a small boy bending down between his eyebrows. I felt it just made me look like a gremlin. I knew there was a way of tampering with it, because certain Hollywood celebrities seemed to have expressionless, almost death-mask faces. So I went to a surgeon in the field and enquired what it was.

'We cut the muscle to the skull,' he said, 'but there is this other solution. It's a toxin called botulism, and it's for tics and spasms in children's eyes. We've been experimenting with it in the glabella, which is the muscle between the eyebrows, and it paralyses it completely.'

I didn't hesitate. 'Oh, shoot me up some, Doc!'

So I travelled to this doctor about once every eight months and had a little dabble. Everybody said, 'It looks ridiculous...' or 'Oh, you monster – you can tell something's been done. I can stamp on your toe and you don't even blink!' Well, look at it now, suckers!

But I've never had anything done to my eyes, and nor

have I had a brow lift. And that leads me to lip augmentation... and that's when things started to go seriously wrong.

I'd first had a piece of tissue inserted into my upper lip in 1992, something called alloderm, which is made from babies' foreskins. They use it in spines, or knees when people have arthritis – it's the tissue that stops the bones rubbing together. It's a perfectly compatible piece of organic tissue. It's supposed to be permanent, but it shrunk inside my upper lip and looked a bit like a wiggly worm under lights.

So I went to this Harley Street specialist to have it removed. And he said, 'Instead of removing it...' – which I could have done myself with a pair of tweezers – 'let me inject under and around it with this other solution that's perfectly compatible.'

He showed me what it was and said he'd had no problems. It was polyacrylamide, an injectable substance that didn't have to be done very often, that was semi-permanent – or so I was led to believe – and totally safe.

Polyacrylamide is what soft contact lenses are made of. Soft contact lenses, the eyeball, mucus membrane, no irritation – so, with the lip, it's fundamentally the same kind of thing – there should be no irritation. It was injected once and I got a bit inflamed but the specialist said it was nothing to worry about, because this injection contained microspheres, which are small balls of the contact lens solution surrounded with collagen. 'We'll inject with its sister product,' he said, 'which is called Outline, which is a gel which will suspend the microspheres.'

He injected me with the gel in 1999, and then, shortly after Christmas, it had been absorbed a bit so he injected a few more times. Then he started to inject about every ten days, because I was getting rapid absorption of the substance. Then he was injecting every five to ten days and then we stopped, and then it would be great. Then he'd inject every five days, and then all of a sudden I sensed something was terribly, terribly wrong.

I started to suffer pain, and there were some lumps in the lip area – round, hard lumps. I wasn't aware of what they were but he started to try and suspend the lumps. Well, my lips were up and down, and I started to suffer pain in the jaw. And the lips got so big that I shot a video for 'Spin Me' – which is the one out now – and it just looked so disproportionate. So the specialist suggested putting an implant in the chin to bring the proportions back – it wasn't something I wanted, but it would cut down on huge amounts of money spent on useless lighting people for useless video directors.

So he put an implant in my chin – a small silicon bag secured in a pocket in front of the jawbone. About eight days later, I was on stage at Gay Pride performing, and I just felt a rip inside my mouth – the chin implant had extruded itself through the incision inside my mouth. I finished the concert, and went back to him first thing Monday morning.

He sent for another one from the manufacturers. I took

five Valium, he put a local anaesthetic in and he replaced it. But, for months after, I felt a strange discomfort in the chin area. I was saying, 'It's not in the right place, it's not in the right place – I've got nerve damage in the chin. Something's wrong.'

He kept checking me, but I insisted on an ultrasound, which he eventually agreed to. But then the ultrasound couldn't pick up the clear silicon bag, but the specialist then assured me with a second opinion – from his brother – that it was in the correct place. I was to find out roughly a year later that not only was it not in the correct place, but it was also sitting on the chinbone – as opposed to the jaw – and he'd put a stitch through it, so the silicon was leaking into the skin of my face and my throat and my Adam's apple.

By now, I'd started to look like a monkey. The specialist said the top lip was too heavy and needed lifting. This actually wasn't the case – it wasn't heavy because it's a weightless gel, but I didn't know that at the time. So he insisted on cutting round the vermilion border of the lip to pull it up, which is a very common operation these days. You see it on so many people on TV, where they just raise the lip up by cutting round the outline of the mouth, taking a few millimetres of skin out and then rejoining the lip. I cancelled it twice because I had a bad feeling about it, but he said, 'Look, I'm so positive about this, we won't even sign a waiver.' So I had it done and I got the stitches in like a moustache. But it wasn't healing. The next thing I knew, the lip started to separate from the tissue and it wouldn't heal. And the holes started appearing.

Then, in February 2004, I'd just done a record with the Pet Shop Boys and a gig with the Scissor Sisters and I woke up in such pain I had to take 18 Nurofen. The pain was unbelievable – I was rolling on the floor screaming. It wasn't just my mouth – it was my entire face. There were holes appearing everywhere, with pus coming out.

I was discharging litres – litres! – of yellow stinking fluid. It just kept coming. I'd just be sitting there and I only had to turn my head a fraction of an inch and my skin would split and this horrible gunk would come spurting out of my cheeks – it would fly over two or three feet. A swelling would appear and my eye would shut and gradually a hole – like a cigarette burn – would come through and then it would just pour and pour. I'd try squeezing it but it wouldn't stop and it poured – towels were soaked, T-shirts were soaked – as in more than three glassfuls.

Then it started to come out of my rectum as well – this yellow slime – and it burned, so I had to have all kinds of tests – colonoscopies. And, when I was walking, it was like my arse was on fire. But it was too acidic for creams, and there was a lot – it was dripping out of me. And I don't mean a small leak – you would have had to insert a tampon to keep it in. And then, when you removed it, the tampon would be completely sodden and it would keep coming. I'm not the suicidal type, but I'd take 20 or 30 sleeping pills a day and hope I didn't come round. I was on intravenous morphine and pethadine, but the pain was still unbelievably intense.

Outline, the injectable solution that was put in my lips, was a gel-like formula that enmeshes with your own tissue, which is why it's supposed to be stable. You create a tunnel to put it in by injecting from the furthest point with a large syringe and then withdrawing, and then each end of the tunnel heals. But it gradually erodes the tunnel, becomes unstable and migrates everywhere. Your body then produces an anti-inflammatory liquid which is yellow in colour, and it tries to flush it out in the contaminating fluid. Then the polyacrylamide starts to cut its way out from the inside, and the holes can't close because the inflammatory fluid just keeps trying to push it out. But it can't be pushed out, because it's enmeshed in tissue.

It also eats its way through your face. It ate its way out of the lip right into the face. It ate its way up, down – completely through my face. It was the same as the silicon disasters in the 1960s, when women got silicon injected into their faces. And Vegas showgirls, instead of getting breast implants, got silicon injected into the breasts, and look what happened. It went to the brain, it went to the kidneys – they died. And I nearly died from what happened to me.

There are no words to describe exactly what happened. There are no words to describe when you nearly asphyxiate in the night because the inflammation travels to your Adam's apple and you can't breathe or swallow.

There are no words to describe how you arrive at the offices of one of the most respected reconstructive surgeons in the world and he says you're going to have to have your whole face liposucked, so you have come to terms with the fact you'll never be able to speak, eat or sing again... and you will be horribly deformed.

You must have seen a liposuction pipe, the one with the huge diameter that they insert into you. They were going to do that in my face. You can't do that – it's too big and too aggressive, but it would have removed the solution, which could have choked me or blinded me.

The holes were eating me up from the inside out, so they couldn't heal – they stayed open. If a doctor had found a miracle way of closing them, it would have come out through the right eye, because it was travelling towards the eye, and then the eye would have had to come out. And then they realised it had lodged in the muscle fibres, and that it had been injected too deep into the dermis so it had entered the bloodstream as well, so my kidneys were trying to eject it. And then, when I started to get my thromboses and an embolism and experience seizures, we were really in trouble.

Now I was facing blindness, kidney failure, bowel failure, nine kidney stones and a thing called a stent installed in my left kidney on a temporary basis. A stent is used when you have a piece of foreign body so large in the kidney that it starts to come down the urethra and they have to take the urethra out and put a rubber pipe in, straight down the penis. I was catheterised for about four weeks because it was causing massive inflammation throughout the rest of my body, including thrombosis of the arms and legs.

The body is a whole thing – it deals with trauma of every kind, and fights it as best it can. It had an alien substance travelling round it and it was sending all of its inflammatory fluid to protect itself. My whole body blew up because it didn't know what was going on. At its height, my face was four times its normal size.

How do you go about getting help for something like this? You use the Internet, and start looking all over the world – no hope in London... no hope in New York... no hope in LA. And then hope from somebody who is a member of the fan forum on my official website, The Right Stuff. Rose Keefe, who runs the website, told me, 'There's a plastic surgeon on here, he's Italian. Do you want me to talk to him?'

I said yes, and then I got a phone call from him and he knew exactly what the condition was because there have been countless cases in Italy. He and his senior doctor, a surgeon, flew over within a week, because I couldn't fly – I was too swollen. They were mortified that this could have happened in this day and age.

The plastic surgeon was a cancer reconstruction specialist. He told me that he could remove the offending material, but I would have to have most of my face removed from its structure, all the toxins would then be scraped out, and then my face would be sewn back on.

I went to Italy, but, when he opened me up, it was

worse than he'd thought. He worked on me for five-and-a-half hours in what he thought was going to be a one-hour operation. The whole recovery process should have taken four months – it actually took a year-and-a-half. In that time, I should have had four reconstructive operations, but I've had more than a hundred.

I had tumours all over my face and my neck, and all of them had to be removed. It wasn't cancer, but the only person who could remove the tumours was a cancer reconstructive specialist who specialised in reconstructing patients whose faces had been eaten away by the condition. He said it would have been a whole lot easier if I had been in a fire or if a hand-grenade had blown up in my face, or if I'd gone through a windscreen.

So the journey began from there. And, oh boy, what a journey it was. I lost most of my lips. I had to have a process called skin flap rotation, and had most of the lip tissue removed. I then had stem cells – I was the first person ever in the world to have stem cells for that purpose. They had to remove my stomach wall, taking all the skin away to regenerate skin, to rebuild and regrow tissue and put blood flow back where there wasn't a lip any more. They had to take a section of skin, bigger than a caesarean, to break it down to regenerate my face with stem cells.

There was a huge tattoo below my belly button with Michael's name on it – 'Michael, you are my love, you are my heaven, it's written in the stars of the day we met' – it was so beautiful. But they had to cut from the belly button to the pubic area, and from hip to hip. I lost all feeling in that area, and now it's rock hard.

There was another hurdle to overcome after that. My mouth was sealed shut – both lips. Some might think that was a blessing! But it wasn't a joking matter. I just had one hole out of the side. I didn't have lips – we had to grow the tissue and then separate it and make it into a mouth. I had to learn to speak again. I couldn't eat, or kiss, or brush my teeth for seven months.

Another factor was that it wasn't just my lips that were affected. It had started in my lips, but then went everywhere – my cheek, my jaw, it was seeping into my neck, and I was suffering major nerve damage. I couldn't speak or eat or drink. I was unconscious. At one stage they were going to remove both lips, and possibly a portion of my nose... I had to sign consent forms to the effect that, when I woke up, they might have had to amputate a part of the affected area – lips, part of the chin, cheek, my Adam's apple, maybe an eye – they never knew. So I'd wake up and wonder... is it still there?

I was under observation for that entire 18 months, seven days a week, because I could have gone into necrosis, where the tissue dies, or tissue rejection. I was having two operations a week, except for a couple of weeks off in August when they took a break.

So that's what I went through with my reconstructive surgery. What a genius my doctor was. I thank God, on my knees, that I met him – and he hardly spoke a word of English! How great – you put yourself in somebody's hands and you're so vulnerable and all they want is the best for you, and they say *'piano'*, which is Italian for 'slow'. It was psychological torture and he knew it was my road to Calvary, and he was surprised that I didn't break down – I just kept going and going. His respect for my tenacity and physical strength and recovery rate moved me on to a whole new level. People may laugh at that, but they've got no idea what I went through.

It's a horrifying thing to happen, but there are thousands of people out there with the same polyacrylamide as there was in my face. My problems didn't happen 'til four years down the line, so it's a virtual time bomb. And doctors still use it in Ireland. Most of the doctors I went to for help were all doing it, too, and they refused to give affidavits on my condition. They were just judgemental, and said it served me right.

It wasn't a case of having too much done – it could happen with just one shot. It happened to several people that I've heard of with just one injection.

And it's ongoing. I've still got some tumours where my lymph nodes are, where it's migrated into my armpit and neck. My doctor says now it could be four years, five years, until the system has digested it. In the meantime, it's got to be stopped from coming out, so it has to be suspended in a natural substance all the time or else it will push its way through again. There are always going to be remnants in my system. It's enmeshed in the tissue, layer upon layer. It's become part of the tissue, but tissue degenerates and so will the polyacrylamide.

I'm under constant supervision every day, with phone checks and medication to monitor it and control the inflammatory process. I had two procedures while I was in the *Big Brother* house – they had to call in a doctor as the show was under way. I couldn't have anaesthetic – I had to do it fully conscious with a topical anaesthetic in the Diary Room and that was no fun.

It's got to go on for maybe another three years, on maybe a ten-day basis. If I do go on tour, I'll have to take a doctor with me, and how glam is that? Some people take a nail agent or a wig-maker – I take a doctor. But it's no big deal, you know. I'm not thinking, 'Why me?' Why *not* me? That's when you move forward and move on – why not me? I'm repulsed by victims. It's a choice. It's not about being a fighter, you don't have to fight to be a survivor – it's a natural state of being to survive. But people choose to go the other way and go down. I'm not fucking going down. When the nuclear bomb goes off, there'll be two things left – cockroaches and me!

The surgery wasn't the only thing I had to endure in Italy – not by a long way. Most of the surgery had to be done in the surgeon's villa because they wouldn't let me into hospital. It's a Catholic thing – all run by nuns. The first five-hour operation was done in a hospital – the Villa Serena in Genoa. After that, they only let me in once for emergency pain relief. My face swelled up to six times its size and I started to lose my eyesight because the inflammation was hitting the optic nerve. I was vomiting and I became bowel and bladder incontinent because the pain was so bad. We couldn't get in touch with my surgeon for eight hours because of the language barrier, and, when they got me to his place, they rushed me to this Villa Serena hospital and I was put on morphine and pethadine and huge doses of Valium, all intravenously.

The final operation which involved removing a section of my abdominal wall and all the various layers of fat. This was in a second hospital, which was available at the right time. I was told to wear no make-up when I arrived. So, of course, I put on all the make-up I could muster, and then I just thought, for my own amusement, I'll put on a black baby-doll nightie so that when they came to take my blood pressure that would really amuse me and mortify them! And it worked – they were all coming in and asking for autographs and giving me flowers!

Putting on make-up is how I live, but another reason for putting on make-up was the disfiguration – the scars were so horrendous I couldn't bear to confront myself. What I had to confront didn't operate within the bounds of public decency, because when I went out in the street, even with make-up on, people shouted *'Brutto!'* which means ugly. It's more traumatic than anything that's ever happened to me. I was covered in stitches. I wore a mask, like a Michael Jackson mask, right through one Christmas, right through a summer, all the time. It was made out of a black Louis Vuitton scarf, but it was a surgical mask none the less.

There was one person who saw an inner beauty and an

outer beauty, and simply accepted that the outer beauty had gone. To Michael it didn't matter, but it did to me, because I couldn't love myself, so how the hell was I going to let anyone else love me? I could let him look at me, and I couldn't look at him. It took me two or three hours to have a bath and I did that every day. I just couldn't face going in the bathroom. I ran away from him, went and stayed somewhere else – I made up all kinds of excuses and lies because I couldn't face him.

Michael's selfless support throughout that difficult period was the most amazing thing, and I thanked God for the luck, fate – destiny – that had brought us together.

During my time in London, I had grown to like Joe Allen, the restaurant in London's Covent Garden. I like the people there, I like the service, I like the room. I don't actually eat a lot, or go out a lot, but, when I do, Joe Allen is where I like to be. And one night there, sitting at Table 26, my life was going to change for ever.

I was with friends and it was late. We were laughing and then I looked up and saw him. His name was, and still is, Michael, although I didn't know that then. I knew nothing at all about him. But I knew, like a force of nature, that I needed to.

Michael was standing at the cash till, working out someone's bill. He didn't see me looking. But something had happened to me. A connection I couldn't understand had been made. I believe in previous lives, so maybe I knew Michael in another form, in another life. Maybe that's why it was like a flashbulb of total recognition going off when I saw him. A cannonball. Every cliché you can think of.

I didn't speak to this man the first time I saw him. I don't think he even saw that I was there. But he was in my daydreams from that moment on. Such daydreams they were, and all I seemed to live for was going back to Joe Allen to feel and feed that electricity.

I worked out that week like a madman, because I was a man possessed – with my life partner. And, when my friends and I had our next Joe Allen meal, I sat there and I felt the same connection. I recognised his face; I knew this man... even though I still didn't know his name.

I don't do girlie crushes. I don't fantasise about teen idols – not when I was a teenager, and not when I became a man. So this feeling wasn't about the façade of the man at the restaurant cash till. I was already beyond that, but I was starting to feel scared that he wouldn't see beyond me.

How many dinners did I eat at Joe Allen, just because I needed to feed off this stranger's energy? No idea. But I would sit there 'til my arse was square on the seat just to see him. And my heart just wasn't there if he wasn't there. I was hollow on the nights when I didn't see him. Lynne was happy to come to Joe Allen to behold the face that was possessing me there. 'Notice me... notice me... notice me... look at me... look at me...' I screamed it, from inside.

I was on the cover of the *Telegraph* magazine when all this was going on. What I never knew, as I sat getting square-arsed at Table 26, was that the man I felt connected to had seen something in that picture. It had spoken to him and he had spoken about it. 'Michael's new boyfriend' – that's what someone had written across the top of the page, ripped it out of the magazine and pinned on to the Joe Allen staff notice board, he told me later. My arse cheeks would have been in better shape if I had known that sooner.

When we first spoke, I was shaking. A man in his forties, as scared as a teenager. I wrote down my phone number for Michael – at last this man had a name. But I wrote it wrong. My mind was shaking more than my fingers. I missed a digit, in every sense. But... this was the night. It was happening. Building up. Not storm clouds. But the same feeling. This was it.

There's a Spandau Ballet song called 'Through the Barricades'. Michael and I joke that it's our song because of one line in it about love being made on wasteland. But, for us, we made our love by waste bins; in the street, outside Joe Allen, by those fucking bins. That's where we first really spoke, outside the rush and the madness and all those faces inside the restaurant. It's such a bleak and quiet street; dark and narrow and tall. No neon, no other pubs, no restaurants or businesses. A single line of road between hard-edged brick walls. And the bins.

'I'm going to a party. Come with me?' Was it a question or a plea? An offer or a demand? I don't know, but I made it. And Michael said no. He was on a break. It was too busy. He had to go back to work. But he said no. And I was a scared, rejected, misfit kid all over again.

I went to the party, anyway, but I couldn't focus. Michael... Michael... Michael. In the end, I knew I had to just leave and go home. And then I got the text. It was 3.00am, I was in Shaftesbury Avenue, and Michael was off work and could meet me.

It was raining by the time I turned round and headed to the Shadow Lounge in Soho where we had agreed to meet. But I didn't go inside. I stood with the doorman, cold and wet, in case Michael got lost, got distracted, got cold feet. I was close to knowing him. I couldn't lose him now.

Inside, we talked, and then we headed on. Around a couple of corners to Balans on Old Compton Street, for breakfast at dawn. We were there 'til 6.00am, maybe later. Two friends of mine were there to check this man I was with wasn't a serial killer, but I reckon I'd seen enough of life to be able to detect that already. I knew Michael.

It was cold that morning. Silver, not grey, in the city sky. I didn't care if daylight came. I just wanted the night to go on. I just didn't want to stop talking to this man I had just met. I had to keep the moment going. 'Come back to my place?'

My life is not about one-night stands, but I already recognised that Michael was not going to be one. That was not what this was about. We weren't going to do beginning, middle and end in just 24 hours. I wanted 24 years. 24 lifetimes.

I seized that fucking moment. We went to his flat, in Oval, south London. It was a small flat, one bedroom. It wasn't my world. But I was out of my world anyway, out of my bubble. I was in his. And I was home.

We stayed in that flat for six days. Six nights and six days. I had no change of clothes. I had a make-up bag and I had never been so comfortable.

Can you really fall in love, can you know someone so deeply, so fast? Yes, if you have the Burns DNA, I believe. My dad and mother had no time and had to speak in a language which wasn't their mother tongue when they met. They were on opposite sides of a world war. But they knew that they would love each other for the next 50 years. So they took that chance and they love each other still, even though one of them has now gone.

With Michael, it was just as easy to love him, because, like my parents, I believe I knew him before I ever met him. In his flat, I realised I knew his hands, his legs, his arms. I had seen it all before, felt it all before. Another world, another time? I don't know. But none of it was new to me. And all of it was right.

But it wasn't all just easy gushing crap those six days we were holed up together. I had drama, too – the panic gripped me many, many times. If Michael went out to the shop to buy cigarettes, I lost it. Floods, rivers of tears, practically scratching at his door like a scrawny, queeny cat. Where was he, why had he gone, why was he not back? And would he ever come back? Had I lost him already? You're in his fucking flat. It's him who has the key to the fucking door. Of course he'll come back. Calm the fuck down.

But still the tears, the sobs, the terror. And the coldness, the sheer sick-making relief when his key was in the lock and he was back in my world, when we were together again.

We both gave up a lot to spend those vital first days together. I cancelled meetings, appointments, friends. He cancelled all his shifts at work. We were the no-shows. We were making room in our bubble. We watched *Cabaret* and David Bowie videos. We found each other.

Spandau Ballet and the waste-bins. That'll make me smile 'til the day I die. But other songs have moulded, measured and marked out my life as well. There are songs I heard and knew, just knew, that they meant something, even if it would be years 'til I saw it. Songs I knew applied to me and the life I was one day going to have. Debbie Harry, Blondie, 'Dreaming', that's one of them. That speaks about finding Michael.

Could I have stayed in a council flat in Oval for more than a week? Not without more make-up. And not with my roots showing. Anyway, Michael and I had a life to start leading, and we were going to start straight away. I headed back to my house, already feeling that it wasn't just mine. Michael came for the weekend. He never left.

I know – because he told me and because I was next to him on the sofa when he was on the phone to them – that friends told him to steer clear. They didn't get me, because they only knew the freak on the magazine and record covers. The relic from the tabloid gossip columns. Michael is years younger than me. He's handsome, so handsome. He's wise, so very wise. And his friends said he could do better than me. He gave up his Joe Allen job so we could really get to know each other, 24/7. But everyone told him: don't give up your home, don't leave your flat. So he kept it on, for a month, I think. But by then our 24/7 pattern was as flawless as I wanted my face to be for him. So he let it go. He hadn't been back for more than ten minutes for all the time he'd kept it on. We lived together by then, in our home, our bubble, our world.

I won't live in fear of what others think, or shout, or throw. I won't compromise who I am or what I want. Michael and I are tactile; I want to touch him. I want the warmth of his hand as I walk. I want to feel his shoulder blades under my fingers while we wait to cross a road. I don't get same-sex couples who walk down Old Compton Street hand in hand, arm in arm, then let go the second they reach the end of it. How can you change the way you feel, and the way you want to live, just by cartography? Why are you different depending on which grid of a fucking map you are in?

So Michael and I don't. We walk a lot and, if we want to touch, we touch. So how come we don't get the hassle people might expect? I think it's another manifestation of what we feel about each other. I think people aren't idiots. I think they only attack things when they think they can do them harm, when they think they can damage them. And I think somehow, on some level, people get the fact that they can't harm or damage us, that we're sound. Too strong, too close. That everything will just bounce off us. Michael and I do live in a bubble. And it's too strong for any other fucker to break.

Michael has put a lot into place for me because I held back a lot on things I liked, because society and opinions made me think 'no'. It's like if I'm writing a song and you said to me, 'That sounds like "Everybody's Talkin",' I can't do it. I've lost it. If you're walking a tightrope and someone says, 'Look, you're 60 feet above the ground,' you're going to fall.

This is the first time I have had a support system. We just fit together – full stop. Physically, I have contact with Michael; it's not clumsy, it's like a ballet, it's so easy and graceful and smooth, everything fits.

People say you need some space and yet Michael's put it into words – he just says we can talk about everything, laugh, cry, argue, shop, read, watch films... but it's like there are so many people within these two people that we really don't have a need or a desire for anybody else.

And now I needed that support system more than ever, and it was Michael who carried me through our time in Italy. I hid as much as I could from everyone around me. I couldn't tell anyone what was happening; I lied. I said I was in Italy making a record. I went into shut-down mode, because I was traumatised. I wanted to die – I was taking overdoses of barbiturate pills before I went on to anaesthesia, hoping that I would go into heart failure. But you know what? I woke up every time. So that plainly wasn't going to work.

It also affected us when we were looking for a flat. We were renting a flat and we were told to try to not go on the balcony because the landlady lived opposite. They would suggest to me, 'Don't go out on the terrace... you don't like the sun.' But we did go out on the terrace a few times and, when the lease ran out, we tried to renew it and we weren't allowed to. So we were homeless.

Then an angel – Marina Zacco – came to our rescue. She's Canadian–Yugoslavian–Italian, and a professor of the English language at the Genoese School of English. She's a fellow patient of my surgeon and teaches him English. When he examined me, he asked her to fly to London to do the translation, and the minute she saw me – she had no clue who I was – she said, 'Listen, you can come and live at my house.'

Marina is a woman out of her time. She's physically in her late fifties but mentally in her early teens – she dresses like Christina Aguilera's grandmother, with tattoos and everything, and rides a motorbike,. She's unique coming from a society like that. She isn't eccentric, but very intelligent, so her intelligence gets her diplomatic immunity from her 3-inch skirt and her ripped stockings.

She lives in a place called Bogliasco, near Genoa, on the coast. When you walk into her home, you can see the ocean and there's beautiful marble everywhere. But it's a tiny place, and she's got two huskies – one's 14 and one's three – and they've never left the building. She lives on the top floor, so she'll take one down in the lift, and then bring it back up again. She loves animals, but she won't let them out.

So we looked for another flat and Marina went to look at it first. We were offered the flat, so we both went to view it and suddenly it wasn't available for six months – only for a seven-year lease. So we said we'd pay the seven years, but they said, 'Oh, no, you can't.' Then we went to another flat. We didn't understand the language, but it was clear that they didn't want us there, not even for a year's rent. The landlord actually said perhaps we should go away and become rich and famous pop stars and 'then maybe then we'll consider you'. I was totally traumatised; I couldn't even get a flat.

So we ended up staying with Marina after all. And how poor were we?

I was in recovery from my operations. I couldn't leave the house. There was nothing in the village. There was just me and Michael, no English TV, no English to read, no magazines, no papers. We couldn't afford to hire a DVD from Blockbuster because that was in the city and we didn't have the money to pay the two euros to travel about. We didn't have shower gel to wash with. We didn't have toothpaste, and I wouldn't dream of using somebody else's because I couldn't replace it.

Michael wore some Nike shorts and a vest and I wore a pair of tracksuit bottoms and a T-shirt and trainers for months – that's all we had. And what were we eating? We were using yoghurt in our coffee. We had to eke out a packet of tiny little bacon bobbles in rice to give it some taste. Tuna was a luxury. We had virtually nothing to our name, but it was down to Marina that we had a roof over our heads and a sofa-bed under our bodies. Thank heavens for small mercies.

Marina wasn't rich by any means, but she used to forward us a few euros each day. If I said, 'Look, Marina, we've got no food, we've got nothing at all,' I could phone Steve and say, 'Look, we need about 20 euros and we need some cigarettes... we need some milk.' He'd phone her, and we'd get 20 euros in our hand. We spent 40 euros once in a supermarket – it was the talk of our house! 'How could anybody spend 40 euros on food?'

I felt really lost in Italy. Michael was with me, though I wasn't with him because I was so drugged and so full of fear. Sometimes, you want to be with somebody so much you drive them away. I didn't know who I was going to be when I got back – or what could I do. How could we support each other? What would we do for money, because Michael had given up his work for me? And he certainly didn't come to me to be kept, because, my God, he's had a hard time. I was quite nasty to him – very nasty, at times, while I was heavily drugged. I didn't remember a lot – I'd be getting a general anaesthetic, then getting it again two days later, and he'd never been through a general anaesthetic so he didn't know what it does – blackouts, and slipping between consciousness and unconsciousness.

After all that, *Big Brother* was child's play – a bat of an eye, a wasp sting on the arse of an elephant.

Having had so much work done, and taking so much pride in my appearance, I know I'm going to stand out, to be noticed. My mask is what protects me from the outside world, but it's also what attracts attention. I have lived all my life with the fact that people feel uncomfortable not being able to place me easily in the right category. It jars with their view of the world that I don't fit. I'm a square peg in a round hole to them. And, underlying the curiosity, they always want to know – am I gay, bi, trans or what?

I say, forget all that. There's got to be a completely different terminology and I'm not aware if it's been invented yet. I'm just Pete. It freaks me that someone could think I was a woman. Don't get me wrong – I love women; I love men, too, and I'm very proud to be a man. It's amazing what you can do with the penis and the anus, so I've got the best of both worlds.

It has been suggested to me that I've had gender dysphoria, because of my choice of clothes. I mean, I'll wear a dress but with biker boots. I'd never wear false eyelashes. I'd never wear false breasts; they'd weigh me down too much. I walk a very grey area, but, if it makes me feel more masculine, then so be it.

I've worked very hard on my body with weights. My ideal body would be LL Cool J's – a huge, muscular, built-up body. That's what I would want with this head – that's the kind of physique I would want for me. I love to wear suits with ties, but then people would take me more for a lesbian dressed that way. If I wear a sheer dress, people can see what's going on underneath and it's my statement. But they don't want to see what's going on underneath. They don't want to see what's there because they're in some kind of denial. I've come to the conclusion, rather like Quentin Crisp, that I'm in the profession of being. My everyday life is a uniform.

From the minute I leave the house, I'm working. Even if it's just to get through the streets safely and to my destination without being interrupted – it's work, so I'm putting on my work suit. Any work suit is drag. Firemen, when they put on a fireman's uniform, are in firemen drag. Policemen, when they put on their policemen's uniform, are in police drag. If it's a uniform, it's drag – it's a working uniform. That's what drag queens do. They live as men. When they work as drag queens, they put on their drag and the artifice. We're all born naked, so anything we do from there in the growth cycle is drag. It's the role we're ultimately playing.

I've been called a transvestite a lot lately but, in the days of Bowie, we didn't know that word. Imbeciles have discovered a dictionary. Journalists have actually discovered there's a computer and they can look up words. I'm not 'trans' anything – I've arrived. I was a poof in the 1970s, a gender-bender in the 1980s. I like the word 'queer'. But, you know, call me anything you like as long as you call me.

It's easier for people to give you a label, because then they have a better grasp of you. They give you a label they're happy with, because then they can go, 'Now we know what he is.' But they're actually just looking at an item, a veneer, a sign – because it's a skirt, in their eyes you wear women's clothing. Do they look at female stars and decide they're transvestites because they wear trousers?

Women don't get labelled like that. But Scotsmen wear kilts, and look at the Ancient Greeks. The Romans wore togas. If I see something nice, even if it's meant for a fucking dog – a dog coat in Harrods – I'll wear it. If I see a nice blanket, I'll wear it as a coat. Whatever I see that pleases the eye, and whatever tactile sensation it gives me, of comfort and moveability, or constriction or no restriction, I'll wear it.

I really can't understand it. How many women do you see who dress like me, or look like me? None! What a sad indictment of our society that, when somebody plays a transsexual, instead of using a transsexual in the role, they use a female actress. Isn't that sick? They're not comfortable with the real thing, so if they perceive me as being the real thing, by their definition, and they're putting me up there in the spotlight, that's fine.

The Beaumont Society – the transsexual society – have condemned me. They made a statement about me in one of the papers, saying I was a disgrace, and a desperate flake. It's a shame, because some of my Big Brother charity money is going to a transgender support organisation for kids, called Mermaids, which is for gender-dysphoric children to educate teachers and disadvantaged parents. You know what? It takes many kinds of beautiful flowers to make a garden.

When people do perceive me as a tranny or a woman, they're picking up on the identity I created that was part of my character as a performer, which is very different from the person that's underneath. So I am being perceived as a character that I didn't create – they have imprinted that on to me – and, if someone creates a role for you, it's very difficult to change their perception.

When I did the Pet Shop Boys single 'Jack and Jill Party' – I love it – a song about homosexuality, I rewrote the lyrics for my 'character', along the lines of a Bette Davis role. Neil Tennant's lyrics were something about being in the palace and counting riches and I sang about being in the cat house – with my bitches. There was also a line I did about beating your face and ratting your hair. Neil said, 'What's "beat your face"?'

'It's what the transsexuals in New York do,' I said, 'when they put their powder on – they really push it on.'

'What's "rat your hair"?'

'It's teasing it up with a tail comb.'

Neil didn't know this terminology, and he thought it was fantastic.

But I wish they'd written 'Flamboyant' or 'Being Boring' or 'Domino Dancing' for me. I want pretty songs. I'm sick of being Cleo the Whip Lady. I'd rather do something with beauty and glitter, but instead I'm doing 'Sex Drive'. It's like 'Here I am... Here's my role...' But, hey, it was a great time and an album was seriously being talked about before my face exploded.

But I'll tell you who does find me attractive. Arab men

love me. I was stopped in Harvey Nichols and they said to the girl on the till, 'Anything he wants... anything he wants.' But I haven't taken it. I've been in Selfridge's shoe department and some rich Eastern person has said, 'Whatever he wants... absolutely everything.' And the shop girls came round and said, 'You can have anything you want.' And I thought, 'I don't want anything.' Not out of churlishness – if I'd wanted anything I wouldn't have thought twice about taking every pair of Alexander McQueen boots in the building.

I like to go walking late at night through the early hours. I used to love that – I explored London for a period in the 1990s that way. I'd go out from my house in Chepstow Crescent, walk all the way through Holland Park, go all the way along through South Kensington, through Knightsbridge, to the end of Chelsea. I'd walk and walk through 'til nine o'clock in the morning. I'd get home, we'd have some breakfast or do some exercise, and I'd go to bed. I'd wake up in the afternoon, then I'd get up at night and do the same. I had space and solitude.

But there was one particular period in the 1990s when things were going a little crazy in my life and I just didn't want to go home. I'd just walk through London, and I discovered all these arcades off Piccadilly and back streets in Covent Garden – secret little alleys with theatre bookshops. And, eventually, that journey led me to a place near my home called Edgware Road. And several occasions I got a substantial amount of money because some emissary would come up to me and say, 'Will you come to this hotel?' and I thought, 'Oh, God, they want to fuck me. They think I'm a hooker.'

'I'm not a hooker,' I'd say.

'We know you're not,' they'd say, 'but King Such-and-Such wants to meet you.'

And, on several occasions, I was ushered into a hotel room, escorted by several people. And all these Arab men would want me to do – and I swear that this is true – was stand in front of them, take a bath, undress and let them see me naked, then get dressed. And I would get a large amount of money and be taken home in a chauffeur-driven car. I did it about six times.

It was easier than a gig – no rehearsal. And it was a lot shorter. It was a matter of three minutes and you were gone, and it was more money than I could get for a gig at GAY... with some jewellery thrown in. And the amount of respect – I was holy to those people! I wasn't treated like a scorned whore – it was as if I was a demi-god, one who was doing them an enormous favour, and they would acknowledge that with a gift. And never once were they in a state of undress. I never went there looking for it – it just happened.

All of us have a skeleton or two in our closets, and I think my skeleton is a lot less rancid than most other people's. We get undressed to have a bath, don't we? We get undressed in the gym changing room. And I really realised the power of looks then. I realised people might have misconstrued how I looked, but I could use it in my favour. And, once they spoke to me, they certainly realised that I wasn't what I looked like. I was fucking sharp, and I never once took a drink of alcohol in those situations. I never trembled and I was never afraid.

And, after that, I met some other people who did it and who lived the life of Reilly. Head-to-toe Vuitton. One in particular was a transsexual prostitute – she's still got her bits – but she doesn't have sex with them. They want to see the titty-cock boy. And she lives a life of style and elegance, and she's a very gentle person. But she can get £40,000 for three days in Dubai – without any sex involved.

People like her – their heads are together; I've spent time in their company, and I've seen how they operate for myself. They are strong, confident people who go through a process of self-transformation for no one else but themselves, and they're certainly not going to allow anyone to fuck with them. You can look, but not touch.

If there had been any sex involved, I wouldn't have touched it with a bargepole. It was just really easy money, although, at the time, I didn't really need it. I had great publishing royalties and fantastic PRS – Performing Rights Society royalties – but, hey, this was big time. To give you an idea, when I did a record with Glam, I got a flat fee of £6,000 – because I wrote the song – and a fur coat for doing that record 'Sex Drive'. It took two days. The other thing took three minutes. And they treated me like royalty.

How did I know I was safe? These are diplomats and kings. I know when I'm safe and when I'm not safe. God knows who they were, but they'd shake hands and bow,

very like the Japanese. I took it slow, and took it clever –
I walked behind people and never let anybody *ever* get
behind me when I went into those situations. I walked
slower than anyone else. And only once did I ever find
myself in danger, and that was when I knocked it on the
head. Strangely, though, the danger wasn't from the
people who paid – it came from outside.

I was taken to a place in Maida Vale – I still see the
house when I drive past it; it's like a palace. Two guys
approached me, and said, 'Somebody would like to meet
you and they would like to look at you and give you gifts.'

'OK,' I said, 'I know the drill. Where are we going?'

Maida Vale in a blacked-out car. So I arrive, and find
them smoking one of those tobacco pipes. I always
checked them out for drugs, those pipes, but there
weren't any – they tended not to do drugs. So I
undressed... they watched... I dressed again... got the
money... and was ushered out.

No car this time. So I walked out of this house in Maida
Vale at 7.00am, and there were loads of schoolkids
around at that time. They followed me while I looked for
a taxi, and I noticed that they all had bottles. So I started
to wonder what they'd do, and decided that I'd have to
defend myself. So I went into a supermarket, bought a
bottle and smashed it to scare kids off. I thought I was
going to get killed, so I reckoned that that was enough for
me. Never again.

12

spinning out of control

'I've got a good sense of humour, but I'm also fairly serious about my career and deeply serious about keeping my self-respect.'

After extensive tours to Japan, the death of my mother and a tour of America, my voice was worn out – in fact, I was completely fucked. I went to see a doctor, because I was just feeling shit, you know. I was given anabolic steroids and I felt great on them, but I ballooned up to about 16 stone, and then they caused terrible depression, but I don't know if they knew that at the time. I started to wake up in the morning in a terrible state – crying all the time – and I noticed that I'd developed a lump in my testicle. I was exercising a lot and I just couldn't walk – the pain in my groin was unbelievable. My dad said, 'Look, we're going to the doctor.'

For me, this was an embarrassing thing to go to a doctor about – they look at me and think I've got a vagina. People find it very disconcerting that I've got a dick and balls – I'm not supposed to have them.

But we go to the doctor, and he does the most humiliating examination ever. The thing with the prostate, squeeze the balls – it was horrible. I felt vulnerable. And they put me in for a cancer scan. I couldn't stop shaking. He said, 'Let me have a look at you.' He made me stand on my toes and everything, and he says, 'Oh, multiple sclerosis.' I didn't know what it was, so I looked it up and freaked out. I thought I had cancer and multiple sclerosis.

But to test for multiple sclerosis – which they can never actually say you've *not* got – you have to get mutant motor-neurone muscle-conductivity tests, go in that scanner, brain scan, needles through the muscles, the works. And, all the time, I was waiting for the results as to whether I had testicular cancer.

I was then looked over by another doctor, who immediately said that he had a bed ready for me in such-and-such a clinic, and that I needed to start this medication – a tricyclate anti-depressant – and it was estimated I'd gain up to seven stone. I was so heavy and I was breaking down and saying, 'I can't do that, I've got to go back to work...' But he just said that there was a bed waiting for me.

I was so freaked and traumatised I was given Prozac, but they weren't making me feel any happier, so the doctor upped the dose of Prozac to three a day... and then I became fucking suicidal. I couldn't function at all; I was in bed crying and my hearing became super-sensitive – if you dropped a spoon it would sound like a cymbal crash. I remember Pavarotti was on in the park and I could hear him through our French windows – the greatest tenor in the world sounded like nails on a blackboard to me.

I didn't know what was wrong with me and I was having more and more medical checks and they were saying it was hypochondria, and then Steve went off and Lynne also left, but I don't know where she went.

I screamed. I screamed for days. I thought I had cancer and multiple sclerosis. This was not a case of hypochondria – I had a lot symptoms, muscle jerks and numbness, and I couldn't tolerate any noise at all. I stayed in bed for more than 14 months.

During this time, I was constantly referred back to the Institute of Neurology, which is in the centre of the West End, for test after test after test, for more brain scans. We then added Parkinson's disease to the list. I developed complete numbness in my fingers, I couldn't hold a cup, so my dad was living in the street opposite with his new wife and he was trying to be hands on. I was going to more Harley Street specialists, the Chelsea & Westminster Hospital, more tests, colonoscopies. They were just so awful, and I had to be carried to and from taxis.

Then, to top it all off, I was sent for an ultrasound. I

was in an absolute state, but they put some jelly on my balls and the woman said, 'This is a varicocele.'

'What's that?'

'It's like a varicose vein in your testicle. It's from not wearing adequate support when you jog. It's really common in men to get this and it's one of the hottest summers, and they're really painful.'

I didn't believe her, so I went and got another check.

My dad said, 'Look, we'll get three checks and then it's finished.'

The three checks were finished, but I still wasn't well – the stress had done me in. I'd been bedridden for ages and, I swear to God, I had bed sores all over me because I couldn't move. Dad would come over and he'd give me a sponge bath, or he'd try and get me into the bath, when both Steve and Lynne, who were with me in the house at the time, were off doing their own things.

It drove me mad, the physical breakdown, and I knew I'd go nuts if I didn't get myself up and out, at least to meet some other people and return to some sort of social normality. So I forced myself out, slowly, gently, and then for slightly longer periods.

At the time, I met a girl who was really into witchcraft. She'd been an editor for the *Daily Mail*, and came from a very rich family. She had an incredible house, which I went to live in for a while, and she was prepared to introduce her whole life to me, driving me everywhere in her huge Jeep.

She was heavily into a book by Clarissa Pinkola Estes

called *Women Who Run with Wolves* and, on every wall facing a window in her house, there was a giant wolf's face. The philosophy is rooted in witchcraft and protection rituals, and is supposed to prevent break-ins if a wolf faces a point of entry.

Well, it turned out to be true, because she'd leave all the windows open – in an area of London with a high burglary rate – but it was never broken into, despite there being a lot of studio equipment stored there.

It was in Stringfellow's that I saw – I swear to God – the most beautiful man in the world. He dropped a drink down my thigh-high boot and I blew up, and he said, 'I'm so sorry, I'm so fucking sorry,' and he was all nervous and he was adorable. I took him to a restaurant in Drury Lane and then he told me that he was a policeman.

I then got a call from Pat Geary, who helped to run my website, who said that I'd got a gig in Scotland for £5,000 and, as I hadn't worked for ages, I took it. So I travelled up with my policeman protector, and we ended up sharing a bed together... but that's *all* we did, as I was so exhausted.

He came to my aid again when the lads from the Ministry of Sound sampled 'Spin Me' without my permission. My policeman checked out the legal aspects, and prevented them from continuing, so then they asked me to go in and re-record 'Spin Me', for which they'd give me £5,000 for the vocal. I thought, 'Fuck it, I'll do it, but I'll make a mess of it,' and I went into the studios with them on the Ministry of Sound label, got my £5,000, but they couldn't use it.

My physical and mental shutdown was imminent, so after all the medical checks, drugs, diagnoses and misdiagnoses, I decided I was fried, completely fried, and I made a very serious suicide attempt. I was convinced I had cancer, multiple sclerosis and Parkinson's disease – I was actually put on the medication for that, even though they couldn't diagnose it and, because of the shakes, I couldn't even speak properly. It was becoming more and more difficult, as I was spending so much money seeing doctors and Lynne was becoming more and more distressed over it all, and Steve was getting anxious, too. It wasn't hypochondria – it was real. My nervous system was simply giving up. You think you've got cancer, multiple sclerosis – you're living that lie.

But I wasn't going to go through the wheelchair shit, so I got Dr Kevorkian's book, *The Final Exit*, and I got every goddamn drug from this friendly little pharmacy. The only thing I didn't do was put a carrier bag over my head, and put a nappy on, because the chances are you'll shit yourself.

Then Steve went away for a weekend and my dad had gone somewhere, thinking I'd be OK. But I couldn't drink the vodka, and I was supposed to take all these pills – two travel sickness pills, a piece of dry toast, his mix of stuff, a load of aspirins to cause a haemorrhage... I did absolutely everything that I could, bar the carrier bag, the nappy and the vodka.

But I couldn't do it, and the next thing I knew, I woke up and I was being hit so hard. There was an ambulance, and the police were there. I remember two huge bull dykes trying to strap me into an ambulance and saying, 'Stomach pump... stomach pump!' But I wasn't going to let them do that because they do it as a sort of punishment. They make sure it's unpleasant so you never do it again, and I wouldn't be taken to hospital.

They went, and then I passed out again, so I was asleep for a few more days. Then I crawled downstairs one sunny afternoon, climbed over the back wall and went to Notting Hill Tube station to throw myself under a train. I was swaying on the platform at 8.00am – I'd warned them I was going to throw myself under a train – but then suddenly something happened and I got to a phone box and managed to dial our number. And the next thing, Steve came round in a taxi and got me out of the phone box and take me home to bed. I got the all-clear, but by that stage I'd had a breakdown, so I went to the Charter Clinic. It was around £2,000 a night and I hadn't worked for a long time.

One evening, though, I went out, and left a candle burning in an alcove. There were some crystals near it, which caught fire – nothing major, and nothing was damaged, but I had a bit of clearing up to do.

Then I heard a knock on the door. It was neighbour of mine and a load of police, and they said, 'There's a fire...'

I told them it was OK, but all of the alcove was burned, and then the neighbour asked, 'What's that lovely smell?'

'Angel,' I said.

'You can smell angels?' she said hesitantly.

'No… it's a perfume called "Angel" by Thierry Mugler…'

And the police then leaped in with, 'Right, that's it…'

I was put in the van and taken straight to hospital. I didn't know what the fuck was going on; I was wearing a Jean-Paul Gaultier sequinned, ankle-length kaftan, I had hair extensions to the floor in purple, orange and green and I had blue contacts in. I went, 'Let me out of here… what's going on?'

'Yeah, yeah,' I was told. 'We'll let you out in a minute…' and there were all these strange people coming to observe me, monitor me, test me… it was like an acid trip, I thought I was fucking hallucinating, and then I hit somebody because they wouldn't let me leave. There were all these corridors, but they wouldn't let me out so I punched somebody and four or five women rushed in to restrain me on the floor.

I tried to fight them off, but I was injected with various drugs used to control hyperactivity or aggression. I couldn't talk for four or five days, I was just drooling.

They kept administering them to me for days, and then I was moved from that secure ward to a room of my own, but I couldn't make any phone calls, and I still didn't know what was going on. I was so angry, but no one would tell me a fucking thing.

Then I found out that a restraining order had been placed on me, so they couldn't release me, but they wouldn't discuss it with me. Eventually, I was allowed out only under Lynne and Steve's supervision for one hour twice a day, and I had to go and stay in a hotel because I wasn't allowed within 75 yards of the house. But I could only stay in the hotel if there was one of them with me. I couldn't even walk into Chepstow Crescent, where my house was; I'd have to return to the hospital by another route. I could walk, but Steve had to accompany me.

I slowly got better, and was told that I'd be allowed home... as long as I agreed to go on a tour of America.

The second time I was sectioned, I was touring America with Steve, and Gina was with me, too. By the time I got to New York, I'd lost my voice and I was feeling ill. I was already on Prozac, one a day then as a maintenance thing.

I was also being given steroid shots, too, and because I'd put on so much weight I was put on a diet pill that reduces your desire for carbohydrates, you just don't want them.

So I felt really tired, and sent for a doctor, who gave me anabolic steroid shots to get me through the New York show, and asked whether I was on Prozac.

'Yeah.'

'Oh, shit!' he said. 'I'm going to prescribe these for you... It's a new anti-depressant. You've got to clear out the Prozac, because this is a different drug group. Start right away, and take these pills four times a day with steroids.' I think the drug he'd prescribed was Wellbutrin.

So I did a great show, started the next day, felt fabulous, met Sandra Bernhardt to start to set up contacts in America, and had some hassle with my dancers. That turned out all right, though, as the show hadn't really been advertised extensively, so we got on with the gig as best we could.

When I got back to England, I couldn't sleep. Christmas was approaching, so I said to Steve, 'I'm in trouble. Get me a doctor to sedate me, I can't sleep.'

'Have a spliff,' he said, but that wasn't helping at all.

So we phoned a lot of doctors, but they wouldn't touch me because they didn't know what Wellbutrin was. Then I decided to stop taking it all together, and forced myself to get out, and back into seeing people, going out, kick-starting my social life. Oh, God, I was so active and I was making loads of new friends.

I performed at the William Hunt fashion show wearing a copy of the Koran as a boob tube with four skirts on and did a cartwheel. I had no knickers on and Richard Madeley, Judy Finnegan and Faith Brown were in the audience and they saw my knob and everything, which wasn't deliberate because I was barefoot dressed in this Indian costume and the last thing I expected was four skirts to fly over my head. I was quite proud of myself, actually.

I was doing OK, but I would have moments when everything just became too much; I'd freak out, and then I'd need help from someone... anyone. I remember getting in a taxi to go to an appointment and saying to the driver 'Selfridges'. The next thing I knew, I looked out and we were at Heathrow Airport.

He said, 'You said Heathrow Airport.'

I didn't know what he was on about; I'd been quite

clear as to my destination, so I freaked out in the taxi, I mean really freaked.

I got home somehow, and I was desperate for Steve to get me some Valium. I was like, 'I can't stop... I can't stop... I can't stop...' and then Steve went out for some shopping, and Lynne took a taxi to her friend's... and they never came back.

So there I was, on my own, and desperate. I didn't know where Lynne or Steve were, so I tried to carry on living the only way I knew how, going out all the time and just trying to drink myself into a stupor. It didn't work.

I went to an all-night bar on Christmas Eve, and I met a beautiful boy from the Cayman Islands. He had green eyes and looked like a model. He told me that he dealt pot, but he was homeless, so I said, 'You can come home and live with me if you want...'

This wasn't for sex; I gave him a room and it turned out he was really, really ill. He had scabies, and he needed treatment for it.

'Look,' I said, 'it's Christmas Day, we'll get some food,' so we went to McDonald's for our Christmas lunch. I also found out that he spoke French, so he made some phone calls for me, and we had Jean-Paul Gaultier ringing up a few times; clothes were being delivered to us; it was crazy.

After a while, he started to say he was confused, because he was having dreams about sticking his penis in me, and I got scared. So I blocked up my bedroom door. I started to feel dreadful, and I went to talk to some doctors in Harley Street about my condition. You can see how bad I looked on a documentary called *A Walk on the Wild Side*... there are Internet photos of me, in which I've got red contact lenses and my face is really gaunt, I've got a fringe, and I was really fucking anorexic because I couldn't hold food down.

They released me eventually, and I remember having to walk home in a paper boiler suit. But I couldn't cope without a great deal of support and care – you know, loving care, the sort that really makes a difference – and there was precious little of that around at the time. It wasn't long before I was sectioned again.

While I was being held in the St Charles mental institution, I had a lawyer fighting my case but I kept failing the tribunals because someone would say something to me about my appearance, and if it was someone in a turban, for example, I'd say, 'I hope your fucking head gets better.' All these really weird people were coming in to interview me, and I failed every time because I just wouldn't play their games. My lawyer was great, you know, and she kept saying, 'He shouldn't be in here,' but it took a long time for me to get out.

I remember escaping once from St Charles with a German woman who claimed she had an aristocratic title. We had a blast, actually, because the 'Lady' was very confused and we'd speak German to each other. She said her husband had gone away for the weekend, she'd try to get into the house and, because she didn't speak much English, they used to put her in the mental institution... at least, that's what I was led to believe.

I knew the Performing Rights Society payment dates and I had a big cheque in the Royal Bank of Scotland, so I pleaded with the doctors to tell them what was going on. All my money had gone, and I needed to get some out or I'd have nothing to go to, and I also had a restraining order imposed on me. But there was a chance of getting some money, and at least checking into a hotel. And they said, 'Don't be ridiculous... you're delusional, you've got no money.'

So I decided to go on my 15-minute jail-break with the Lady. I was with a nurse and I pushed him straight through a bush. He was out cold so we jumped in a cab and we went to Notting Hill Gate, where I got a lump of money out. From there, we went to a hotel, because the police were after us, and she booked us into a room and we ordered up a load of room service.

Then we wanted to go shopping, but the Lady had lost her credit cards, so she got on to the front desk and placed an international call to her husband, but she needed to nip outside for a cigarette, so she missed it.

The next thing I knew, we'd hopped in a taxi and we went over to her husband's grand house, to which she had a key, but apparently they'd changed the locks. He was away at the time, and we got to the Lord's doorstep, and then we get into the house because the servants think she is his wife. Only then I did realise, 'Hold on, hold on a minute... something's wrong here...'

Well, it turned out that she'd never even met the Lord!

It wasn't long before the police pulled up and I was taken back in, and they thought it was a right old hoot.

I was then put in the secure ward with the schizophrenics and some very, very dangerous characters. I was physically attacked by a schizophrenic, who nearly broke my neck in there. I attacked him back, but then I was put in solitary confinement for four days. It wasn't much fun. I'd rather have fought the schizos. But the discipline of the mental-health system in this country is wonderful! You stand in the corridor on one leg with one arm in the air for an hour or you get no food. I ain't standing on one leg for anyone! I went through the whole gamut in there.

In the end, I was just discharged. It was absolutely unquestionable that I was fine. Other medical experts were brought in and said to the doctors in charge, 'This man is 100 per cent well.'

'Then why is he standing round in a kimono with full make-up on and an Adolf Hitler moustache at seven in the morning?'

That's exactly what I had been doing – I'd put full make-up on. They'd go on about make-up in the morning and the fact that I had a black kimono, and they found that objectionable, so I started to put a Hitler moustache on with all my make-up every morning and they thought that was a symptom of my insanity.

They also said I was trying to have sex with all the patients – men and women. There was one patient, in her fifties, who was obsessed with cancer and dying, and she'd cry constantly in fear. I'd hug her to comfort her, you know?

Eventually, I was just discharged. I was in for a lot longer than the statutory 28 days. I kept getting additional time, because there was the restraining order and I was homeless with no money, so I had nowhere to go. It was a long, long time.

So, from the depths of despair, to hope, and a saner future. Michael has been an integral part of my recovery. Ours is a unique kind of love – this is what I believe love should be, but, then again, I think it would be very rare for anybody to feel the kind of love that we have between us. I don't think it fundamentally exists any more, because people won't let it in and, if they've got it in them, they won't let it out. People are emotionally and spiritually constipated, so they don't know how to express it.

He expresses his love for me in poems and just in physical contact, and he's letting me have the wings that I need. If I wanted to walk in here in a ballet tutu with a rapist hood, he wouldn't question it – he'd say, 'Well, why don't you add some clip-on earrings?' He understands that me wearing what's deemed a female dress is nothing to do with being a transvestite – it's fabric.

'We are not going to give Pete Burns women's clothes to wear in a men's magazine.'

Why?

'Because we don't want to encourage cross-dressing.'

Oh… so if Kylie Minogue phoned up and wanted a man's suit?

'We'd give it to her.'

Why?

'Because she's Kylie Minogue.'

So it's very acceptable for women – right back to God knows when. Look at what Dietrich did with trousers – banned from the streets of Paris when she wore trousers, and all of Dietrich's suits were tailored by men's tailors.

But then Dietrich was sex without gender. She didn't look like she'd spread her legs and be a goer in bed. In fact, she looked liked she'd stand up straight and tell them, 'You get down on your knees and you are lucky to be there.' People found her to be a real sex bomb, but she wasn't vulnerable, like Marilyn Monroe's desperation.

They didn't call David Bowie a transvestite then, because they didn't know how to spell it. But, you know, I can buy what I want and wear what I want, and this is like the childhood that I never had. I've always looked at things, but I can't have that because people will get the wrong idea. Well, sorry – the person who matters most to me certainly doesn't get the wrong idea. And he just adds things to the mix for me – it's just so thrilling to have someone in your life like that.

13
guiding lights

'I swear to God, I'll have to go and get a colonic tomorrow – my arse, you could open a bottle with it!'

I have alluded to having an ability to see beyond the natural, physical world, and my first personal psychic experiences started during Mother's illness. I was watching *Dynasty* – this was months before the diagnosis – and the word 'cancer' flashed up on the screen, brightly coloured. I've still got the VHS tape. Then, when my mother came to visit me, there was a grey shadow over her left shoulder. I thought it was like Vaseline or something in my eyes, but everywhere she went I could see that on her back. I had no clue it was cancer and I kept saying to Lynne, 'She's gonna die... she's gonna die,' and she was like, 'She's fine... she's fine.... she's fine.' My mother eventually went for tests – and she wasn't fine.

Before this, in Liverpool, there had been signs. When I was a child, there used to be a TV show called *The Outer Limits*, a black-and-white series set in outer space, and I used to have recurring dreams about being inside a spaceship. I knew what the inside of a spaceship looked like – the console, the window into outer space – but the spaceship I kept seeing myself in had a lot of balloons in it.

Many years later, when I completed the recording of *Sophisticated Boom Boom*, I realised that the recording studio looked like the spaceship I'd seen as a child, and the balloons were there to celebrate the end of the recording – I very clearly remember the balloons, all pink and yellow.

I was an avid reader so I used to get comics, but my father was a bit mean at the time, so the comics were always two weeks behind, from a place called Salomon's in Port Sunlight, a shopping area called The Wiend. Eventually, after I kept getting more and more old comics, he got me a delivery on a Saturday morning of a comic called *Tell Me Why*. It was an educational comic, and you sent away for a free atlas of the world. I had a big map of the world as well, and I pinned it up and used it to throw darts at. I kept hitting Japan all the time, and I had a recurring dream of being in Japan, in a really old place which I couldn't possibly have ever seen before. It turned out to be Kyoto, the oldest city in Japan, where the Japanese record company put me in a really special hotel where I could look out from the terrace. And it was exactly as it had been in my dream.

Later on, in Liverpool with Lynne, there was a mirror opposite my bed and I could see the duvet and somebody underneath it really in pain. I thought it was Lynne, but then I realised it wasn't my duvet that was in the mirror. I phoned home and my mum had been rushed into hospital that morning with breathing problems – this was a long time before the cancer. I'd not been there for a long time, but I saw her duvet and everything in the mirror.

My mum had psychic abilities. She didn't say, 'Oh, there's a ghost upstairs,' or anything like that, but we had a lot of disturbances in Port Sunlight, which I'm quite sure my dad would verify.

There was a long period after my dad's mother died in the house. My grandmother hated my mother. She had bowel cancer, but Mother nursed her through that, and there was the most tremendous crash in the house just as she died. We rushed upstairs – I was a child – and she was dead in the bed.

After she died, my brother's girlfriend, who was a model – was at the house, living in Tony's room. I was sleeping in my mum's room and my dad was in the room that his mother had died in. And all of us, unanimously, would hear somebody running up and down the stairs in the night and the living-room door banging. Everyone would meet on the landing – I was very young at that time – but something clearly wasn't right.

This went on every night for a long time. One night, my dad waited on the stairs. I was in bed but I couldn't sleep and then there was the sound of running up and down the stairs with such force that everyone got up. As soon as the lights came on, it would stop.

We checked the house for mice, but mice don't usually wear biker boots. Things became so unsettling that, on several occasions, Mum would just take me from the house in the afternoon – whoosh, we were out. We'd spend hours out in the afternoon in the winter and not go home until tea-time when Dad would come home from work.

I do remember, very clearly, coming in one afternoon and Mum going straight upstairs and saying, 'Christ! You are *dead...*" and standing in front of the door to the attic, which had been completely opened. It was impossible to open it, yet it was open. And, in the room my nan had died in, the door was wide open and the bedding had been removed from the bed and the curtains had been taken down.

And then I remember a priest from St John's Parish, and several other priests being brought in to cleanse the house, but it didn't work. And then on another occasion, a neighbour was going past the sitting-room bay window on a winter's evening, and she started to knock on the door and became quite hysterical – 'Souls are in there! Souls are in there!' She was trying to push her way in and my dad was going, 'Calm down, calm down!'

My mum got a bucket of water in the end and threw it over the woman, because it was like she was tripping out, really losing it. I thought it was terribly exciting that my mum went and filled the big bucket with soapy water and threw it over one of our neighbours!

After a while, it abated and then it just seemed to stop. I was a kid, and I didn't know any fear, so I wasn't afraid of those kinds of things at the time.

There were many more strange incidents. This man called Caspian was seen – not the alter ego that Griff used, but a spirit version – and he'd rotate lamps in the room. Paul Rutherford was there one night and each lamp just leaned right over him, very slowly, and then they went right back up and then the curtains would rise up.

Pat and Liz – the two girls Griff shared the flat with – would find their clothes shredded, like with a razorblade, in the wardrobes. Griff would go into his room and there'd be three cigarettes lit and burning.

I was in Griff's flat one morning – and you must remember I didn't do any drugs or anything at all – and I was ironing. There was a whole box of matches, and each match was thrown at me in the kitchen, while Griff came in and watched what was happening.

On another occasion, we came in and Pat's valuable art deco teapot collection was smashed. There were other shelves, one of which had paperweights on it, but none of the others had been touched, and nothing had fallen on them. We photographed all of this.

Another incident occurred when I went into the bathroom, which was outside the flat, and the bathmat was pulled from under me.

We knew when Caspian was coming – the clocks would stop. So, just by a certain stillness, you'd know he was there. He'd generally come when there were a lot of people there, and anyone who came round knew Caspian would probably be there, too. It wasn't predictable but it was very obvious when he was there – like when Paul and Lynne stayed in the living room and the curtains were raised. I said 'Hello' to him – I just think he wanted to be noticed.

Tony Kildare was someone who worked for me in my clothes shop and he had also experienced disturbances in his house. I had photos of a dog growling and an imprint of a man's face in someone's skirt. We all spent a lot of time in Tony's house. Often, a cat would come in – but there was no cat, yet everyone would see it. It wasn't exclusive to me – these things were making themselves very, very visible.

Tony also experienced somebody knocking on the door, so he went downstairs. When he came back upstairs, the curtains had been removed from the window and they were laid under the mattress – they'd been perfectly folded, and the bed had been made. Also, he woke up one night when we were there and the bed was sopping wet, although where he'd been lying was bone dry. You knew something was there – you could see it, like I had seen on my mum, like a mist that lingers. But it wasn't all over the whole room, it was confined to a specific area.

After losing the flat in Holland Park, after Mum's death,

I got a house in Chepstow Crescent that I really do believe had been cursed. It was the unluckiest house in the world for me. You could buy the rug of your dreams and you'd put it on the floor and it'd look like a beer mat. You could buy your favourite picture – I've got an original Biba picture that means so much to me – and I could put it up on the wall there and it looked like an Athena postcard. You got the best of the best in that house and it just looked incredibly insignificant. The doors would stick. Everything went wrong – no hot water, no heating. It was as though the house was saying, 'I just don't love you.' And we tried to love it, but it was a bit like an unruly child, so we needed to get out. Even when people came to view it, it was on the market for nearly two years and, although it's beautiful, no one bought it. It was strange – it was almost as though you'd walk in and you'd never want to leave it, but, when you did leave it, you turned a corner and you never wanted to go back.

It had a history, that house. A property developer bought it from a very old lady and he let her keep the basement. He lost his business so we bought it at auction. Several people – my current partner, Michael, included – have said in the back room – where *nothing* works – that she's in the house. Somebody came round who had no psychic ability at all and just said, 'Who's that old lady in the back? She's really pissed off,' and they hadn't known the story. But the telephone wouldn't work, the Internet would go down, the cat wouldn't go in the back-room area – it was just a very cold part of the house.

Many years later, I was angry that my mother had died when she did, while I was in America. I was angry that I never got a sign from her, because she said she'd give me a sign. And, once I'd bought the house, with everything that went on in there, I'd wonder where my mum was.

One day, I was in the house in despair, and I'd just come out of hospital, and a postcard that she'd sent me many years before from her holiday – I'd put it on a bookcase – fell down. 'I love you and miss you, Mutti,' it read. And then, quite a few years later, out of the middle of a book came a postcard – 'You are music, Mutti.' She had such beautiful handwriting.

I was never allowed photos of my mum in the house, because Lynne used to say she scared her – creepy, dead people's photos. So, when Michael came, I sold a lot of clothes and we got a pile of money, and literally overnight we transformed the house.

Because it was Christmas, and Christmas is the most special time for me – always has been – we rushed to Habitat. Michael's very much into the same décor as I am, so we revamped the house. We bought these deep wine-coloured bed covers and we threw them over sofas. We bought a Moroccan table and we sawed the legs off. We got tiny little rose fairy lights and put them around the huge mirror. There were candles everywhere. We had a lot of red velvet roses – oh, it was so beautiful, that house...

And we got out all Mum's photos, and we went to Oxfam and bought loads of those ornate silver frames. Every Polaroid of Mum, her childhood photos, her father when he was young – I'm the living embodiment of Mum's father – everything all there. And every night I would light a night light and I'd talk to her and go, 'Mum, I've got Michael. Thanks for sending me Michael,' and I'd sit and talk in the early hours of the morning 'til four, five o'clock.

But then the money ran out after Christmas. I couldn't sell anything – I had nothing left to sell. How bad was it for money? We didn't have money for cigarettes. We'd wake up, no cigarettes or newspaper. But, OK, we're clearing up, and there'd be cigarette boxes in the alcove by Mum's pictures, and there'd be money in the box – like £20, a fiver and some coins. And Michael would go, 'Oh, Pete, there's money in here.' And I'd go, 'Well, I didn't put it there.' And he'd say, 'Well, I didn't have it, so where did the money come from?'

It was odd, particularly as we were finding money in – well, we called it a shrine – to both of our mothers; family pictures and things. And it just kind of progressed, you know? Literally, someone was helping with money. We would have checked every single pocket. You know when you've checked everything twice, the inside pockets, the ones that are zipped up – you've checked just in case there might be a fiver there? Well, one day in one of the drawers – again, on a bad day – we found an envelope with some money that definitely hadn't been there. We'd both checked those particular drawers. And it was more than a few hundred. But it hadn't been there, it wasn't in an envelope we used, it wasn't in a place where you'd put money, it wasn't a place where money had been – it was just very strange.

There was definitely magic happening there, and it wasn't just me going nuts – Michael was witnessing it, too. I felt so relieved, because I've always been sceptical of what I was seeing and what went on around me. But he'd also seen this money arriving in weird places, like an old cigarette box, and we'd count the change, bag it and take it to the bank. We'd have something like £50–60, and that'd be a lot for us at the time. Then, suddenly, all the all-night shops would let me take loads of things away. I'd walk in and they'd go, 'It's OK, pay us another time.' Eventually, you feel too embarrassed to go back in and get more. But we were living. We were struggling, but then, at the end of each day, something would appear.

Now, Gordon Smith, who's a world-famous psychic, has come on board. He's in his early forties, and he's been on psychic TV shows and exposed many of them as frauds – he's walked off live TV. He thinks it's cruel and it takes advantage of people, but he's absolutely real. He'll text me – 'Something's happened' – and he's right, it has. Gordon has opened so many doors for me. He has said, 'There's a sword in your life and it's going to cut out all the negative, toxic people. You're surrounded by drug addiction, alcohol abuse and manic depression. There are people in your life who have become completely toxic and they're reacting very badly to the energy force around you and that's why some people are terrified and can't do anything – they just run. There's a sword coming

A promo shot done by James and James with digital retouching by Gozra.

The results of the problems I had with the plastic surgery on my lips – I want everyone to see what happened.

Michael has taken some of the most intimate shots of me – gazing out to sea (*top*), together (*bottom left*) and with Michael's daughter, Jezebel Star (*bottom right*).

This was the night I went into the Big Brother house.

Top: That 'gorilla' coat which caused such a fuss in the *Big Brother* house.

Bottom: Doing some robotic dancing with MP George Galloway.

Left: In March 2006, Michael and I went to see the *Basic Instinct 2* premiere.

Right: Michael and I at Miss Great Britain 2006.

Opposite page: Michael took these shots of me in the hotel we stayed in after *Big Brother*.

Promotional shots done by Michele Martinoli with digital retouching by Gozra.

into your life and I see some potentially very upsetting texts from several people.'

Soon afterwards, I received a hostile, psychotic text from a very close friend – 'You are a fucking joke. You fuck with your own family – don't fuck with mine. You fucking wanker and that rent-boy twat boyfriend of yours...' I hadn't spoken to him since the day I came out of the *Big Brother* house – I'd been too busy – and then this came through.

When Michael forwarded all my texts to Gordon, his view was: 'This is really happening and you must not be afraid... There's a sword coming into your life and it's not your choice, and it's cutting a lot of people away.'

And what was on the wall the other night? A light in the shape of a sabre. I moved the light and it stayed the same.

More strange things have occurred as well. I had a Dietrich CD on while I was in the bathroom and I nearly had a heart-attack. There's a song she did called 'Peter' and the CD stuck on a phrase – it was going 'Peter, Peter, Peter, Peter' over and over again. I played it to Gordon and it didn't stick. Gordon said, 'It's your mother – she's trying to let you know she's around right now.'

Gordon will sit and have a conversation with you, and he's talking away and then he goes, 'There's a silver haze around you right now – that's your mother,' and it's really weird, the way he does it. And he gave us a real cleansing therapy, because there's so much crap going on around me, but I've still got to conduct myself like the

Queen – inside, though, I can be raging about something. Sadly, I've directed this rage at the wrong people a few times, namely Michael, and Gordon got us through that. We had the greatest healing, just by opening ourselves to the force that we can feel but we can't see. You can't see perfume when it's sprayed in the air but you can smell it. There are senses beyond our understanding. My skin's sore, my eyes are bleary – it's not tiredness, it's like my senses have become clearer and my vision's altering.

I've had several psychic experiences throughout my life and on several occasions I've flipped with fear, and I've met people who've known this and they were trying to tell me something and I've not listened. Well, I'm listening now. It's both of our mothers, both German, both Evas, both just trying to say, 'We're here now.' And nothing bad is going to happen to me at all – it's taken all the fear away. Because, when God closes a door, he opens a window.

I've never tried things like regression but I know where I've been, and if they tell me anything different I'll know they're wrong. I know I've lived in Berkeley Square, and I know that it was at the top of a particular building. I know that I have lived in Egypt because of the repulsion that I felt when I went to the British Museum – it was palpable. Digging up the bodies in public – it just really freaked me. I just know those things. So, if a regressionist said that I've been a fruit farmer in Billingsgate, I know he'd be wrong.

When Gordon came and sat with me, he didn't do a

reading – he just had a conversation and, occasionally, he'd go straight into things and he was so right. So he confirmed for me what I already knew. I would never call Gordon up and say, 'Hey, Gordon, shall I wear blue or green today?' It's a matter of listening to your inner voice, not doubting your intuition; and there's so much white noise that we can't hear our own intuition. It's about shutting out the noise and, in the environment I'm in, I would never hear anything but noise.

There's a wonderful movie called *White Noise*, with Michael Keaton, where he tries to contact his dead wife through Electronic Voice Phenomena and becomes obsessed. Just as I was about to do it, a warning came up, so I'm not going to do it. It comes with a serious warning from the Psychic Society, saying that 87 per cent of the voices that you hear are overtly hostile.

Mike Stock could tune into characters and get them. I heard a record today – 'The Love I Lost' by Sybil. He's the one doing the backing vocals and it's like a lady's voice. All the girl backing vocals on my album – like 'Come Inside' and 'Save You All My Kisses' – that's him. He could just channel voices eerily. Mike Stock was just breathtaking, and the way he'd write words – he'd talk about a particular person, and the sorts of things that have happened to them – bingo! – down with the words, such as the lyrics in Princess's 'After the Love Has Gone' and 'Say I'm Your Number One'. He could just do it from a woman's perspective – always from a female perspective – with every emotional undertone in the song.

Some of their songs were so beautifully written, like 'When I'm Good and Ready' by Sybil, or 'I'm the One Who Really Loves You' that Mel & Kim recorded. Sometimes, you'd get a girl singer in and she'd sing and then she'd go out, and then he'd do the singing for her... and he understood every nuance of the emotion. It was incredible.

I haven't tried séances and things like that – I've no real interest in that. With the spirits, my view is that it's a case of don't call us, we'll call you. There are a lot of them around, and maybe, when one wants a voice, it's as though you're picking up the phone for someone else. The signs aren't there – it's just not cool really for me right now. I've seen séances in a spiritualist church that were just a complete pantomime, and I've done the Ouija board when I was younger, but I just don't want to open that channel right now. I might leave that door open and let the wrong person in. I feel very protected at the moment by things that no one can penetrate – I feel very, very safe. Then, sometimes, I think this is crazy, you feel so safe you must get worried, and I become worried about *not* worrying.

I'm so used to fear and anxiety, but it was not *my* fear or my anxiety – it was other people's fear and anxiety. I realised that, because the chances are that I will live to be very old – but I'll probably look better than Joan Collins! I just want to be surrounded by people who don't make me fear or doubt. I do think there is a negative charge in the world or in the universe and, sometimes, when things are so good, other forces and other thoughts come in. I don't want any friction.

I haven't turned into a 'Zen' person at all, as I'm sure you know by the things that I'll say to people. I'm completely un-Zen, but people ask me questions all the time and they *so* don't want to hear the answer. So it's best for me to remove myself from the board of directors, really. I don't think or judge very often unless I'm just bored, and then I'll play like a cat with a ball of wool. I don't spend an amount of time thinking about what other people are doing, what they're saying, or what they're thinking. I haven't read any of the magazines that are brought in. I haven't read a book in a long time, because I really don't want any opinions right now, except what comes organically.

14
big brother

'I must admit that occasionally I've been really irresponsible
in interviews. Like when once I got a real jerk pushing about the
nuclear bomb… I said I thought every home should have one.'

When the *Big Brother* people first got in touch, Steve told
them, 'No.' I told Michael and he went, 'You're crazy, you
should do this,' but I said, 'Look at me, I'm mutilated.'
Michael's view was: 'You've got to get out there and let
people see.'

I was in hospital on this particular day having a major
operation, but Michael had contacted the *Big Brother*
people through the Internet, got the number and, a
week later, two producers flew over to Italy. So they
were obviously interested and it all kind of snowballed
from there.

213

I asked them why they'd chosen me and they said because they thought I was lovely. I thought they might have thought I was a car wreck, but then when they met me they obviously realised I wasn't and I kept feeling like a crashing disappointment because I didn't act in an eccentric, off-the-wall way. I said, 'I'm too psychologically sound for this, aren't I?'

They said, 'No, no, no, we love you.'

God, I needed the money. Because I wasn't lucid, Michael dealt with the entire contract and I got a really good deal. Plus, because the producers of the show realised that when I came back to England I had no home, they were kind enough to put us up in a luxury suite at the Sanderson Hotel for a month, ending on the day the show ended. What I was looking for was to be out of the house after a week, to be in the Sanderson for three weeks and to have time to go looking for a new home, because I would still have got the same fee.

I felt like I was dying in Italy. I felt like I was going to rot there because I couldn't leave. The doctors were like, 'Oh, you can't leave,' and I understood that, but suddenly the contractual commitments, Michael's nurturing towards it – 'You can do this' – the desperation for money... all of it helped me to heal so fast, I was up and out. I can pull myself together when I have to, and I did. I exercised intensely when I was advised not to. I look now at the stress factors in my life – divorce, house sale, bankruptcy petitions, tax bills, nowhere to live because the house was being sold, no possessions with me because it was all in Italy, the day before Christmas Eve, can't get anything done... but I didn't feel that stress – I threw myself into it totally. And, after being in Italy, *Big Brother* was a walk in the park.

I had no real expectations of what it would be like. The only thing that I went in thinking was: 'I can do this, and I've got a whole lifetime to regret it.' But I don't regret a second of it, not a damn second. I mean, look what it's brought me. The energy force around me is huge. It was very strenuous but it was nothing compared to the period in Italy. It was just another three weeks and there were no operations, there were no drugs. At least there were people around me who spoke my language, as objectionable as most of them may have been. It was fine.

I'd worked it out within days. It's phoney... it's set up. It's sort of psychological torture. It's worked out by a team of behavioural psychologists, and we've all got a role. It's like *Who's Afraid of Virginia Woolf?* times ten, and they're gonna fry us 'til we jump into that role, and then edit the jigsaw that suits their needs. I was very aware of that – I saw the clips and I think it's a genius edit. It's sort of like a Woody Allen film but nastier – *Who's Afraid of Virginia Woolf?* directed by Woody Allen.

It's cause and effect, because you can get great television or great interviews or great pictures if you remove the cause. You know, in the days of Sean Penn, a paparazzo shouts, 'Madonna, you fat hairy slag!' and, true to form, Sean Penn punches them – great picture, but you never get to hear the photographer. A journalist asks you, 'Don't you think Morrissey is rather vile?' and you go, 'Well, he is kind of...' and the headline is 'BURNS THINKS MORRISSEY IS VILE!' Everything is cause and effect, and I'm now only really learning that that is so in life. I'm not innocent – I've caused things that have been bad for me and also I've responded in a way that's brought more negativity.

But it wasn't hard. I just kept thinking, 'Today's nearly over.' I marked the days – I didn't count forward, just day after day off the scale. It was tiring, it was strenuous, and the last 12 days were just awful emotionally. For somebody who was a pampered water lily, it was very cruel. I'm not, but some people in there *were* very fragile.

Michael Barrymore was one of them. You know what he's been through – we don't need to drag that up – and he's suffered with addictions and alcoholism and the death of his ex-wife and being outed. And his whole life has been like this – it's been a snowball that's rolled downhill and got bigger, and he lost his career. He's a delicate personality, and putting him among people like Jodie Marsh with sleep deprivation and lots of alcohol around is potentially dangerous.

I must say, though, I was gutted that I wasn't evicted early on. I totally thought, 'Oh great – I'm out, I'm out!' And I did think I'd die without Michael – I just felt lost and directionless. But I was in for the duration, so he got to live like the Sultan of Brunei in a beautiful room in a huge suite and I was in that nut house.

Why didn't get I evicted? Well, the nominations were from within the house. It was the other housemates who were nominating me and the public just went, 'No.' I'm not in a position to analyse it. I just know that, from other people's perceptions, and the behaviour that was going around me, to certain housemates I represented a real threat – to a lot of the women and Preston particularly. I think he just wanted to be the pop star in there and I had no respect for him. I spoke my mind to him a lot.

I never heard such a load of shite as Preston doing some fifth-grade Madness song, pulling Morrissey poses and acting like a 'working-class queero' as I called him, with 'love' and 'hate' tattooed on his potato toes and him the nephew of Earl Grey. His parents are rich and he's acting like, 'Yeah, Dad, I'm in the trenches,' with his street-cred tattoos. It was like Little Lord Fauntleroy, with his dermatological products and his facials that he used to go for and his back wax and his recent Botox. I saw him on TV and, I swear to God, you could have kicked him in the stomach and he wouldn't have blinked.

As for the women, Rula loathed me. She kept condemning me for my cosmetic surgery, and I kept trying to explain to the silly old bitch that it wasn't cosmetic surgery – it was reconstructive. And she said, 'Well, serves you right!' But at the same time, she was asking for skin creams, and did I have any addresses of surgeons who could make her look like 35 again? She said to me once in an argument, 'I'll never see you again. Actually, I will phone you, though, because I want the address of those clinics that you know.' She was obsessed. And then, as soon as she left, she got in touch with Westwood to get them to dress her, but they said no.

Traci Bingham was typically Los Angelene. She had a sitcom 'in development' and everything was lovely and wonderful. I think fundamentally she was intelligent, but I think most people from Los Angeles are intelligent. They have a sort of animal cunning. I think she was misguided to do *Big Brother* because all she was anxious to do was get her sitcom placed on Channel 4, and to get her billionaire boyfriend to marry her, which he refused to do. It was all very, very strange.

And she had a really bad drink problem. She was drinking three, four glasses of wine before she woke up. She wouldn't admit to any plastic surgery. I kept asking about her hair extensions and she said they weren't. But by the second week, she was scratching her head as though it was flea-infested, because you can't wash those kind of hair weaves. And I was saying, 'Traci, I know what it is – I'll show you how to wash it.' But she wasn't having any of it – 'It's my own.' Of course it was her own – she'd bought it! And as soon as she was out of the house, she was like a robot with her PR guy and she had her own hairdresser and make-up artist flown in from LA. I don't know what was wrong with all those people.

Jodie Marsh – I hated her guts. And there was no point in trying to point out to her what she was doing, that she was manipulative, that she wanted a sympathy vote… she wouldn't listen. Even when she was evicted from the house, it was: 'Oh, January's a bad month for me because it's the fourth anniversary of my best friend's death! And, when I came down the red carpet, they told me that my dad was ill!' He had a tummy upset. 'No, no, you don't understand... they've got an emergency number to contact me in the house if he dies!' What was wrong with him? He had food poisoning. And the public booed her.

Her story about her best friend's death was odd, too. As she said herself, no one at the funeral knew she knew this girl. But she got up and made a speech, and the press just happened to follow her. And, apparently, she'd bought her mum and dad a big mansion? Her mum and dad are multi-millionaires – she lives at home with them.

'I'm ambassador to five charities... I'm against school bullying.' But yet she was a bully herself – slagging off Jordan, saying she was ugly, that Peter Andre wanted to fuck Jodie, that Jordan was going to divorce him, and that Jordan held up her pregnancy test on the front of *Hello!* magazine – 'She'd do anything for money, she's a filthy slag.' They didn't put any of that stuff in the highlights.

'What does Jordan look like?' I asked her.

'Oh, God, she's really ugly from the side. She looks like a witch.'

I just said, 'Don't you realise what you've just done? She's probably got a column out there...'

'But I didn't say it in an interview,' Jodie said. 'I'm just saying it in a house with some friends.'

She was somebody who suffered terribly from

psychosis. I mean, everyone I've met does say that about her. She's half-crazed. She's unbearable. She got Barrymore to shout at her and she went, 'I'm crying,' and it was like Gloria Swanson – 'I'm ready for my close-up.'

And she kept describing herself as 'an authorette'. She had ambitions of being the next Jackie Collins. She wrote it all by hand in pencil – she got really upset because there were no pens, and all the time the words *flowed* through her – she could have written a novel in there, something like 80,000 words a day. She knew every clip and everything she'd been in, full pages, and exactly what they said. I just imagine her surrounded by TV screens and magazines and it's just agony. All I know is, in her presence, I felt nauseated.

But there's no need for me to enter into a war with her, because she's harming herself all the time. Her parents are highly irresponsible for not having had her sectioned under the Mental Health Act and administering electric-shock treatment and cutting her tongue out. That's it, enough, finished – flush the toilet.

I don't think Chantelle saw me as a threat. I think she knew I was on to her, though. She was always pulling poses in the mirror. I said, 'You know that too well. You're not an innocent little ditzy.' And she had cold eyes, and I said on several occasions, 'You're a cold-eyed shark. You know what you're doing and you know you're gonna win.'

And she was always posing with her breasts and I'd say, 'Show that to Preston,' and she was, 'What do you mean?

What you mean?' She took no interest in us when we got out. Her persona had changed completely and she was surrounded by handlers and people to carry her Tesco lipstick and stuff. She's probably a nice girl, unlike some of the people running her life, but, to me, it's glorified prostitution. She seems so young and I don't know anything about her, but then I saw all the pictures in the newspapers – tits out, legs spread. A Paris Hilton lookalike, she said she was. She's more like Paris Stilton!

And she knew Jodie as well. They clocked each other that first moment. They'd worked the same circuit – Chantelle had done Pirelli calendars and things in Britain, so Jodie had to go because she recognised her. Jodie would have given it away.

Were there any of the contestants I actually liked? Michael Barrymore, for all that he learned and is prepared to pass on after the problems he's been through. I think Michael Barrymore is a teacher of sorts, who's been through it all, and come out the other side. But he's had to work hard at it; it's a constant discipline.

I've been surrounded by alcoholics most of my life in one form or another, and by people with addictive natures. And I've been addicted to their addictive natures, thinking I could cure them. And it's often ended up violently and has been upsetting, but I couldn't remove myself from the situation because all the alcoholics I was surrounded by were in my home, so I couldn't leave. But should I ever have the luxury of that going on again, I would have another place to go to and remove myself from the situation. So, consequently, I'm addicted to alcoholics.

Addiction is not just alcohol – it's anyone who has an addiction to anything that's fundamentally destructive. But I have this idea that I can stop them, and I think by bullying them I can stop them, but you can't – you've just got to go and they stop themselves. You can't do it, and that was very much what I was learning from Barrymore. And, when they do stop, it's never for ever because they're only one drink, one cigarette, one shoplifting spree, one pill, one line away from relapsing. Barrymore was like a broken bird, but he was like a phoenix as well – he was rising. I don't know if he got what he was rising for – I don't know if he got a new show. I didn't follow it, but he proved himself in the public eye and it proved that the public doesn't automatically swallow trial by media.

George Galloway was fabulous. I know they edited him to look an idiot because various people said, 'What a wanker!' But, to me, he was a mentor, a tutor, deeply politically aware of everything, aware of human behavioural traits. He told me of a message that was passed on in wartime, where the first person said, 'Send reinforcements, we're going to advance,' and when it reached the end it had become, 'Send three or four pence, we're going to a dance.' And that totally summed up society these days to me – it said everything.

He explained about the Bush administration and the Clinton situation, politics in general, disregarding the black votes – it was like a book that I'd needed to read but I just wanted the meaty bits. Human behaviour, manipulation, morality and his encouragement of me to be a singer – a great singer – his total acceptance of my appearance. He said to me, 'There's only two real men in here, and both of them wear dresses.' He meant me and Dennis Rodman.

And he offered his house for as long as we needed it, and he offered to do anything and to write a Foreword for this book, so, hey, what do you know? I'm not exactly Marilyn Monroe and he's not Bobby Kennedy, but he's good enough for me.

So do I have a new interest in politics now? Life is politics; existence is a political issue; corporate business is politics; the music business is politics... everything is political. So no, because it is what it is and, ultimately, we are not the ones with the power. People don't have a voice, just like talented musicians and creative artists don't have a voice. It's out of my control. I'm only interested in what I can fundamentally control and politics doesn't affect me either way. So tax goes up, tax goes down, council tax goes up, unemployment figures are higher – what can I do about it? I'm basically unemployed, aren't I? I'm self-employed and it's precarious at best. So it doesn't affect me – I've had bad times, I've had good times, but I'm still here.

What would I have done if I'd been given the task George Galloway was given, to act like a cat? I'd have done it. What have I got to be ashamed of? You've got no idea what I do around the house. Last night, Michael and I were disco dancing with a wig head and a portrait. We had a party, just the two of us, and we laughed and laughed and laughed. You do these things. We all have a laugh. I dress up as a nun sometimes and sing a version of 'How Do You Solve a Problem Like Diarrhoea?' *'How are you going to fit that in his rear? How will you catch his cum squirt in your hand? What if he isn't gay? We'll bugger him anyway? How do you make a straight man understand?'* We do things like that all the time.

And I totally approve of Dennis Rodman – fabulous human being. He's been an outcast all of his life. You have to know his life story and about the abandonment of his mother and living in a project, homeless, and his problems with drugs and poverty, and how he elevated himself, and being taken in by a white family who had never seen a black person before. But that's his story to tell. And he's moving things forward in that sports jock culture, because he's so big and so intimidating that they've got to accept that he makes them think.

You'd never see it on camera but I got to know him reasonably well. I got to listen to his background and his life and his views. But, on camera, he was just portrayed as a grunter. He's a slow starter and no one had the time to listen, particularly Rula. He started to talk once, to say, 'You know what? When I was 19... on my 20th birthday I got a $20 and a note my mother had left and I had no home.'

She went, 'Yes, we know. Anyway, darling...' and she started her Zen chanting. She was chanting for all the wrong reasons. She thought a chant was a cash machine. She was about as Zen as barbed-wire roses.

What did I like about Dennis? I was his prison whore for a start – he kept stealing other people's cigarettes to give to me! He respected me. No one would mess with him because of the size of him and yet he was a real gent. Like I called him Fluffy, and hit him and kept him awake all night and threw water on him and things. Because... he was just a free being. He's free and he doesn't understand the power of that freedom yet, because the world is full of wonder for him. So what if he peed in Madonna's vagina and he wrote a book about it? It was very graphic in the book, but I thought his book was fundamentally very interesting. It turns out that he's written five books, whereas Jodie Marsh has written one, and the sales dropped right through the bottom of the lavatory bowl when she came out of the house. No one bought it any more, which I found a bit surprising, but then again how many people actually need a fuzzy-felt book called *Keeping it Real*?

And Faria... I never said a damn thing that they printed about Faria in the paper. I said I missed her every day because she had a lovely energy. I went out with her. How lovely is she? She's a pure soul who's been caught up in a media storm, not through what she did, but because of what other people leaked to the press, taking her emails and bugging her phone and following her. She's a Muslim, and she was just used as a kicking post, and they hounded her mother in America and wrecked the family, just because she fucked somebody and he happened to be a football coach.

We all fuck somebody – it doesn't matter what the job description is, does it? Would they have made as much fuss if she'd fucked a binman? So she just performed a basic human function, she slept with somebody, but it got leaked for other people's motives, to distract from other problems. She's innocent and pure, and good on her. Next time, she should fuck a whole football team and enjoy it. But charge them for it at the turnstile!

Maggot? He was a presence. I loved his records, and he wasn't offensive in any way whatsoever, which is more than I can say for Jimmy Savile. I actually thought he was dead – and I've still got no reason to believe otherwise! I hadn't slept in three days and there was no food, and when I opened the door I thought it was Barbara Cartland. I got so disorientated. I wasn't that aware of Jimmy Savile – I thought he'd been dead for years. And all we got was: 'I met Elvis... I met the Beatles... Aowoo awoo awoo, guys 'n' gals, guys 'n' gals... I'll fix it for you!' God!

When I asked for that thing with Michael, they did a video – which they'd already done before the letter, which was strange. And Jimmy Savile went, 'OK, there he is with his, er, pal...' I went, 'My boyfriend.' And he said, 'Yes, his pal... Lady, boy... boy, lady... aowoo awoo awoo...' He was very uncomfortable around me – 'We don't want to talk about any of that, aowoo awoo awoo...'

What didn't the public see? One thing people always ask me is how I always had something new to wear when

> DEAR JIM.
> I WOULD LIKE TO
> BE ABLE TO SPEND A MINIMUM
> OF ONE HOUR IN A ROOM,
> IN THE FLESH, FACE TO FACE
> WITH MY BOYFRIEND MICHAEL
> SIMPSON. I AM MISSING HIM
> SO MUCH, IT MAKES ME
> FEEL ILL. I AM ALSO VERY
> WORRIED ABOUT HIM, AS HE IS
> A LONER, AND WITHOUT ME
> I AM SCARED HE WILL FEEL
> VERY ISOLATED.
> I JUST WANT TO SEE, TOUCH
> AND SPEAK TO HIM, VERY
> MUCH! P.S.
> THIS WISH IS TO BE
> CONSIDERED FOR YOUR
> FIXING WHILE I AM IN
> THE HOUSE.
> LOVE Pete Burns

This was the letter I wrote for Jim to fix it when I was in the house.

I turned up with such tiny bags? Because our suitcases were delivered to the house separately, of course! I'm not carrying a case, honey. Not in heels!

People also wonder why I said, 'I will kill,' in the Diary Room when I came into the house, about there being no lock on the toilet door. Well, I was in the toilet taking out the stitches from my stomach surgery, trying to dress it.

The space was minuscule, and I only had a small sink, boiling hot water and no lock on the door. The *Big Brother* people knew this – they knew what was wrong with me when I went in. All I demanded was a magnifying mirror so I could see properly in the toilet. There was no lock on the door, 11 people, and the other toilet was out of order all the time.

When Jimmy Savile came in, they knew I was in the toilet taking out an internal stitch that ran the entire length and they said, 'All the lights off in the toilet!' I had to leave the toilet and go to find a dressing gown. I was bleeding underneath my dressing gown, pouring – I had a towel around my waist.

But, when I was in there, all Rula Lenska wanted to do was get into that toilet – she would not stop. She's trying to get in there and criticising the surgery, but then asking me if I could get her an appointment with my doctors and what can she have done. I'm like, 'Fuck you!'

The minute she got out of the house, what does she do? Call up Vivienne Westwood to dress her for my eviction and they said no. But she told Faria, 'Oh, they were phoning me up to dress me.'

Preston's been in there, too, with a stylist and a manager, trying to get clothes on discount – no. Chantelle has even been in. What's that about? They condemn and attack me – but they want some of it.

Oh yes, that business with the police and the fur coat! I realised something was going on outside, but I only got distorted stories about it. I was thinking, 'How can the police do this with a fur coat?' They said to me in the Diary Room, 'Oh, but they would have come into the house in the night,' and I thought, 'Fabulous! Imagine waking up to a big handsome policeman come to take my fur off me!' It would have made better TV than the Sex Pistols boat party.

So, despite all the opportunities to add to the shock element, *Big Brother* stopped it and gave the coat to the police. I find it really difficult to understand that old ladies on council blocks in east London, who are getting terrorised by children or muggers, have to wait four hours for a policeman to show up, while the police managed to run round to grab my fur coat. They think it makes them look really powerful, but they look like total shit-heads.

People say I must have known that the coat was going to cause trouble. No, I didn't. They use the things for vivisection, so what are they going to do with the skin? What do they do with the pelts when they've pulled their eyeballs out for mascara testing and shot them shitless with drugs? What do they do with the pelts, just burn them and pretend it doesn't happen? That coat is old, it's antique, and it was a gift. I didn't choose it – Michael bought it for me. My mother had monkey fur coats; I see no reason not to. I know what they do, but I can't stop it – it's there anyway, so buy it.

People go on at me about the fur thing – what about sweatshops that make trainers and nylon tracksuits that little girls make up for a bowl of rice in cramped, filthy conditions, and sleep on floors? What about the human race? I know damn well what they do to animals, but I also know damn well what human beings do to each other as well. And, if you're in constant denial, you can't help anybody until you've helped yourself. Only when we've sorted ourselves out can we concentrate on wildlife and conservation. We need to serve ourselves, love ourselves, but we don't – we hate ourselves and we start loving everything else.

Karma is instant. It's not something that comes around, it's cause and effect. People think, 'Oh, save a monkey, I've got good karma.' Fuck off. OK, your kid is dying of multiple sclerosis, you need a new drug – what's it tested on? A monkey. We have pointless wars in Iraq, and you get angry over a fur coat? Deal with that, shout louder, march stronger, refuse to go, don't be in the Army, say, 'No, I am not going.' But no, they don't think. They see a fur coat and it distracts them from their own thoughts.

We eat animals, animals eat plants… it goes right down the chain. Plants are alive, vegetables are alive, but they don't have a voice. Do the girls in sweatshops have a voice? Do Nike and all those firms give them a voice? Do they? Do they tell us where all that shit's from? If we don't want fur in society, don't make these prints that make it more desirable. Then don't allow us to have real flowers – we can only have plastic flowers. Oh, it's just ridiculous – I'll hang myself on this subject. That fur coat, that's my fucking war medal. Everything that I've got is a war medal because I really have been in the trenches.

It was Jodie Marsh who instigated all of that. I've got

that from very good sources. She's now trying to get Traci Bingham removed from the People for Ethical Treatment of Animals campaign in America because Traci wore one of my fur collars to do an impersonation of me, not knowing it was real. What kind of scum is Jodie Marsh? Jodie Marsh comes over as spiteful, vile and ugly. I've heard she's approached me to do some kind of commercial with her. If they pay me enough, I'll do it – yeah, fine, I'd be stupid not to – but it doesn't change my feelings about her. Some people might say that was hypocritical, but it's the money they're offering. It's all about money now. I'm getting older and I don't want to be rolling round the stage in a G-string when I'm Cher's age singing 'You Spin Me Round', because, one, it'll drive me crazy and, two, my arse will be round my ankles.

One man that the public never sees on *Big Brother* is the psychologist. Nice man, a good man. He was there all the time, whenever any of us thought we needed him. We talked in the Diary Room – he was on other side of the wall, so you couldn't see him.

What would surprise people most about *Big Brother*? The house looks different from on telly – it's a lot smaller. Mostly, it's how hard it actually is, how cruel psychologically. Deprivation of food, tasks to do for food rewards, but the tasks were for a prize and always the prize would come in increments. There were copious amounts of alcohol and a bowl of jelly sweets. Sugar, alcohol, starvation and bright lights equal psychosis.

All of those people – the civilians, like Jade Goody –

who go in it, they deserve every accolade, everything they get, everything. So I say go for it, because, if you can stay in that shit-hole for three months under those conditions, you are grounded. Go – even the losers win, because the first one out sells all the stories. It's *not* desperate and, yeah, life will be easier. Look how everyone loves you on the street. I've got blue-collars, grandmothers, grandfathers, grandtrannies, granbangers, children, dogs, ponies, water buffaloes – they all love me and they congratulate me. Cab drivers go waving, 'Pete, you were great!' I remember reading this book about Marilyn Monroe walking through Times Square and all the public and the binmen and everyone loved her, yet Hollywood hated her. And I feel very much like that in the music industry.

Fans do say, 'I love you, really. I've just been to Virgin but I can't get your album. Have you got one?' I was wheeled out of a hospital in Italy in a wheelchair – I had drips in and everything – and they were asking me for albums! They just think you carry your albums around. People go, 'Can I get your autograph? Have you got a pen?' I know it's a crush on the street and people lose their mind and you can't berate them, but they must realise how stupid they are at times.

But they've been great, too, because they wiped out the Popbitch website, which printed a story that I had been sectioned in a secure ward of a mental institution after being arrested by the police wearing a glittering evening gown and gluing a pair of Manolo Blahniks on a car in Portobello Road. I didn't even have a computer then, but we got phone calls. The people over the road, who'd seen me every day, were asking Lynne, 'Is he in? Is he all right?'

One morning a couple of years ago, I heard Lynne scream. She was going on holiday and I heard this horrible sound. I ran upstairs and her mother had died suddenly. She was in white-hot shock. Her mother had died literally overnight and the phone was going and journos were asking, 'Is Pete in a psychiatric institution?'

'No.'

'Bring him to the phone – prove it.'

And then Lynne was at the funeral and her mobile phone went off and it was some of those people.

So I got someone to trace *The Face* editor and his girlfriend who ran Popbitch and got their home numbers, and their parents' home numbers, and we posted them on our website and linked it to all the other celebrity websites. They threatened to sue us.

We said, 'Take it off, then.'

'We'll take it off next week,' they said.

'Fucking take it off right now!'

That was on the Friday and by the Monday it was off. But you know what? They got in touch with me and said, 'Will you play at our party?'

But then I got that lovely full page in *The Face*, and they said some really nice things. I was promised a four-page interview, which they wouldn't give me because I wouldn't let a stylist or hairdresser anywhere near me.

But they gave me one page, and that was probably only because that guy tried the Popbitch thing. You see, you fuck with me, and I'll fuck right back with you. And sometimes it's best to let someone deliver their blow. Deliver all your blows and, just when you've run out of steam, I'll give you one back. I think that's the best way of dealing with it.

15

pete, will you please leave…

'If it looks odd, it's ugly. Normal blokes could find [Boy] George quite attractive, y'know, "She's a bit weird, but she's all right…" whereas I'm too extreme. They'd say, "Ugh! Look at that dog!"'

When I came out of the Big Brother house and everyone booed, people said I must have been upset. No. It was like the beginning for me. I mean, who stands outside the Big Brother house in a puffa jacket at five o'clock in the afternoon and gets the last train home? What the hell for? And they wouldn't stop booing! And people were like, 'Are you upset? Are you upset?' I still think people thought I was doing a Quentin Crisp, but no. It was great! I've still got it!

We all grow, don't we? And, as we grow, we get more desperate. When you're young, you've got everything at your feet – as much sex, booze and fun as you want. As you get older, the recovery process is not so quick and you slow down. So everything you do needs to be aimed at achieving the biggest reward. There's no time to waste. So how could I have done any better than *Big Brother*?

I'd like to really thank the *Big Brother* producers. It was absolutely fantastic and I was paid very well, and now I'm in the position to pick and choose exactly what I want to do. I'm not greedy – I could have done everything that was thrown at me and come out with a bag full of money, but all I want is one house and enough money just to eat and do what I want to do. So it was great.

It was a bigger reward to me to be actually chosen than having a Number One single or anything I've ever done. To be chosen and deemed suitable to be exposed to the public and be invited into their living rooms seven nights a week, for what seemed like five years, with no overt censorship – what can I say? They took what I was always led to believe was a huge risk to allow me into the homes of the viewing public, and the music business hasn't really caught up with that bit yet – nor has live TV.

I just know when I walk out on the streets I'm in no danger, no threat, except from too much adulation, because you can get a love hangover. Oh, it's lovely because they want to tell you how much they loved you, but it's overwhelming because you can't go and buy a toilet roll. You're walking round with clinkers and wind chimes on your arse because you've got no toilet paper because you're so busy kissing and hugging people!

Michael and I met a welder who'd seen me on *Big*

Brother and he was in full drag. He said, 'I live in East Bumfuck and I saw you and I thought, "Fuck it – I'm going to do this." I've given up my job as a welder – I went for a week like this – and I'm just going to become my own painting.'

'Power to you,' I said, 'but not only in the night-time, honey – go do it in the daytime. And don't answer anyone back – just keep walking, and know exactly where you're going when you're walking.'

It was amazing. I mean, he'd never have passed as Helena Christensen but maybe it's the start of something. It is the age of Aquarius after all. I think there is a new acceptance, and I've been on the receiving end of that. And if I can help to generate any more of that, for people to follow in my footsteps and just be themselves – and let other people see them being themselves – then that's great. Toleration means there are certain boundaries – 'We will put up with you as long as...' – but it's wonderful to meet indifference, because then you're invisible.

Something else that's been pored over since my stint on the programme has been the surgery – I just don't get it. On the one hand people think, 'Oh, you had surgery to attract men,' and it does attract some men, but it also gets a lot of hostility from women.

Michael and I were out in a club and some guy sat opposite me, and his girlfriend suddenly ripped a strip off him. Later, I was in the toilet and these two women were talking about me – 'Oh, fucking hell, what a monster... How could anyone spend a hundred grand on plastic surgery and look like that? How pathetic! Oh, God, he looks fucking repulsive.'

So I listened to all this while sitting on the toilet, and then I came out and went, 'Hi, girls!' And then one of them came and asked me to have a photograph taken with her on her mobile phone! But the things they were saying about my appearance were just unbelievable. In a former life, I would have been burned at the stake or tied to a ducking stool.

I'm a good person, and I know I can't expect special treatment for my goodness – you don't give to receive. But I don't even receive. I get stuff taken away from me and doors closed in my face still, in 2006.

We can't bear it when things are displayed at their brightest, fullest rainbow colours. We can't bear it, but, when it's gone, we love it, because it's suddenly safe, it can't come back or change. It can't rise up stronger. It ain't going to happen to me, even if I go and live in Billingsgate and own a wool shop. I've got a loud voice and, if you don't want the truth, don't ask me. I'll always have a voice and I'll use that voice when it's appropriate.

I haven't watched the show – I saw the clips when I came out and that's enough for me. I don't really need to see it because I did it, but some old friends have reacted very badly. I can't really see them now because, when I see them, they're going to talk about the show and I'm sick of talking about it. I'm getting texts from people now asking who the fuck I think I am – well, I'm just me. I haven't changed. They must have thought the notoriety or regenerated fame would automatically place me on the red carpet, get me invited to all sorts of celebrity hangouts, and I'd be out drinking and dancing all night, every night. I could, but I don't – all it's done is give me the luxury of identifying opportunities that I'd like to make the most of.

And I cannot tell you the amount of money I have been asked to hand over to all and sundry since the moment the doors slid back when I left the house. I had a friend who sobbed, 'I'm four months behind on my rent and I haven't even sold the story on you.'

Somebody called me up when they read about me buying our engagement rings. They felt that they had to let me know how devastated they were, and that they needed to go on holiday to South Africa but they couldn't get a bank loan because the credit cards were overdrawn. And how dare I buy those ostentatious, vulgar engagement rings, and they needed £600 to get their hair done. I'm not often stuck for words, but that just about does my head in.

I'm just hoping the madness will die down, because I can't see any of those so-called 'friends' again since they've come asking for some readies. And I'm not angry about it – they are. It's as though they've become possessed by demons, they've been so bitter and resentful. So I've had to go into total seclusion until they sort their heads out.

It wasn't just the money. There were several acquaintances before the show who started on my relationship with Michael as well, saying that we wouldn't survive it, that Michael wouldn't be there for me when I got out, and that the only reason I was continuing the relationship was to go on the telly and say, 'I am a freak, and I am loved, I am loved.' They also said he was only in it for the money and the fame.

Well, I let them have their say... so here's mine. Michael and I – we're cool. End of.

What else has changed? People now say I'm brutally honest. Before, I was perceived as bitchy. Now I realise that I'm the one who's living in the real world, and it's other people who can't face reality. Ultimately, the truth is reality. I thought I was in cloud-cuckoo land, but I realised through mixing with the people in the Big Brother house that they're much more detached from reality than I am. You know, the lifestyles that certain famous people live – the valets, personal assistants, stylists, the 'my people call your people', the PR companies – I realised that I never really used any of that. Ultimately, my perception of people in showbiz had shifted; I'd perceived them to be quite grounded and I thought I wasn't. I realise now that I'm much more grounded than them.

They were all so friendly and sociable in the house and at the going-away party, but the minute that ended they were all off with the PRs and hairdressers and make-up artists flown in from LA – Traci Bingham; Rula Lenska; Chantelle with her hairdresser, make-up artist, mother; Preston with his stylist, his A&R man, his manager, his manager's PA, armies of people surrounding one little guy. To me, it was horrifying, because you're just a tiny little dot in the middle of so many dots and, really, you're the food source on which all the locusts are feeding.

I've seen bits of *The Osbournes* on MTV and I love them, but I'm starting to wonder how real that was. I've heard so many stories now about people I've perceived to be genuine – because limo drivers, van drivers, management companies and PR people talk. You can't really be sure if it's not all an act, just a well-crafted and well-edited simulation.

I've always had this theory that showbiz is a perpetuated and generated front – it's a shield from reality. I'm currently in negotiations about a reality show, a fly-on-the-wall documentary. I'm not afraid of that – put it out there. If people want to see it, that's great. It's one thing to show your life on screen – your *real* life – but it's quite another to be surrounded by five cameramen with a sort of itinerarised day, doing things that you'd never normally do. 'Well, we think on day one you'll go into the recording studio and then have an argument with the producer, and then you travel across London and you do the remix. Then we show you, like, designing a cover, and then you go to the hairdresser's…' That's not how my day is structured, so it's a false reality.

But everything now is a false reality, from imagery and photographs, to mascara that artificially extends the lashes, false hair, extensions… Where does it end?

We're now living in a society where even the hairbrush

that a famous hairdresser uses on a famous celebrity becomes desirable – famous, even – in its own right. I actually really loved Victoria Beckham's first album, but it was dismissed and didn't sell because people placed more value on the handbag she was carrying, or the shoes she was wearing. Suddenly, the wrapping, the surface, had become more important and attractive than the object it was covering. If you go to a designer store and you buy a basic white vest, the same one you could buy in Top Shop, the wrapping will be spectacular. But the basic ingredient is just a plain white vest, and I think that is true of celebrities and fame these days.

Big Brother has opened so many doors for me, because I think I was perceived as the 'Spin Me' boy for ever. I started to believe that I could actually talk, that I had valid opinions. I'd always been led to believe by other people's attitudes towards me that I was ugly, stupid and knew nothing about anything. Eventually, like persistent rain on canvas, that attitude starts to seep through and envelop you. The result is low self-esteem, and you just accept it – that's what I am and I'm just vacuous, and, if you scratch the surface, there's nothing underneath. And I did feel that.

There were good reasons for doing *Big Brother* – I've wanted to write, and I'd love to have a chat show. I really would like to have a warts-and-all chat show called *Nothing Special*, on which people could be themselves. Being vitriolic wouldn't work – I'd actually be nice to the guests – but I would knock the PR office out of the frame, and I would invite the Americans on. They can be themselves, but they're led to believe that they can't when wheeled in front of a camera.

If they started playing ball with me, I'd kick the ball. And, of course, that would scare certain people away, but consequently we'd only get people whose motivation and honesty was pure. There are probably a lot who'd turn it down. So that's fabulous, great – bring me the real people and it'll be fabulous.

I'd like to write. I want to do a book on cosmetic surgery – not an exposé, just a source of advice or information. I want to be able to advise people, because cosmetic surgery these days is practically mandatory and I think it's frightful that a lot of these doctors can't deal with the consequences of what they do. There's a race for the new, and sometimes the new is not always really that good, because it's not been tested for long enough and it's a very dangerous area to step into. There aren't enough safeguards, and there should be some kind of new form of medical insurance that will cover reconstructive surgery or complications.

What I'm particularly against with all of these plastic-surgery programmes is when they don't show the pain and the suffering. They show the end result, but they don't show the reality of the process that's involved. It fucking hurts!

I'm very eager to do something else. I'd very much like to do *Pop Idol* because these kids should be careful what they wish for. If you really do want that, then know what you're going to get and be able to deal with it. The thing I find abhorrent about those shows is that it's not only the winner who wins, but the losers win as well. Whose idea was that?

What I'm craving now in life is to meet people who can teach me something. That's always been a part of my outlook on life – I don't want material things from anyone. I want knowledge, and if you can't tell me anything, even if it's about a book or a perfume or a flower or a country, then you've got nothing to give me.

I want a new start. I want to look how I feel. I want to look as good as I can, and make a fresh start, like a flower just coming into bud.

The future? The immediate thing is to have a home for us two – a gilded cage, because I can never go out into the world anonymously. I want Michael to grow and flourish. His gift is photography and creativity. He's done pictures of me in harsh daylight with no performance – just click, click, click, following me around. Best photos I've ever seen, and without all the paraphernalia of the lights, backdrops, entourage...

This moment in time, for me, is best summed up in the Beach Boys' song 'Disney Girls'. I break down when I hear it, because every lyric of that song is me... us. Art Garfunkel has an extra verse in his version, but it's better sung by Mama Cass who sings, *'Guess what? I'm in love with a boy I've found...'* and I'm thinking, 'What else do I really need?'

This isn't a case of J.Lo and Ben – we're not a cliché,

we're real. No one's going's to get between us. But we know they'll try.

I can't say that the divorce from Lynne has been easy – Lynne has her journey and I have mine. We see each other, but suddenly she can't relate to me. She's got her divorce settlement, though, although I walked away with next to nothing, because of the medical bills. My £1.75 million house – I got less than £100,000 when everything was over.

Because of the costs of my reconstructive surgery and my divorce, I've had to sell everything – I own nothing, really. I'm very sad that I lost the catalogue, but I would have been a hell of a lot sadder if I'd lost my face or my life. And with renal failure – which I went into – you can lose exactly that. So it was a choice between life or songs, and I chose life.

Now I've got life, I choose money. When I get money, I'll have a nice life, because there's no going back for me. I've got nowhere to go, because I'm so prominent. What am I going to do? Work in Sainsbury's? My nails are too long.

If the Queen abdicated, she couldn't go and get a council house in Shrewsbury, could she? She'd always be the Queen and, to all intents and purposes, I am the Queen, but don't try and push me off my throne. Just ask me and I'll make a bit of room for you. You're welcome to it and it's a big throne, so there's room for everyone. I'd rather sit on the floor anyway.

I guess there are two worlds – there's the civilian world and there's the fame world, and I'm in no-man's-land.

I'm in a third world and I'm really happy in this world that Michael and I created. I really have never had happiness like this before. But I kind of feel like I deserve what I'm getting now – this relationship.

We do bicker and we make mistakes, like any other couple, but, unlike other couples, we now have certain limitations on our life. This is new to him... and it's new to me as well. The life before Michael, two-and-a-half years ago – that was another existence entirely. This has been like a reincarnation and every minute is precious to me. Even if I drop dead tomorrow, I will have dropped dead really happy.

You must understand – I've got 30 years left, so I don't want to waste a minute. I want to feel everything, see everything, smell everything, taste everything.

My desire is only for a home in an area that I'm safe in, where I can walk into the West End – that's all I want out of all of this.

And, when I do go out now, I know I'll meet fans who want a photo on their mobile phone... and I know you can sell that for £250 somewhere, so everyone's on the make. If you're going to take a photo, I'm not going to pose for it – I'm not Nelson's Column! I'm just me and you've seen me for years, walking the streets – you've honked your horn at me! You've called me a wanker... a tranny... a freak! And now you love me because I've been on the telly.

I'm not bitter... I'm just me... and I've always been the same.

Unique.

16
mouthing off

'It shouldn't matter so much... it's only me speaking. I'm an empty vessel making the most noise. I'm not averse to making a few cutting remarks about myself either, you know, but some people prefer to believe the other version – they like to think I can't open my mouth without making a bitchy comment.'

I'm not afraid of telling people what I think – you've probably worked that out by now. I'll shoot straight from the lip, and you'd better be prepared to hear the truth – good, bad or ugly.

I haven't always had the opportunity to say what I want, when I want, and to have my voice heard without someone shouting me down, or distorting the facts. Well, this is my moment, and I intend to make the most of it.

Well, I've got the mike now, and I've got stuff to say.

The music business has given me a chance to meet and work with some inspirational artists, and I'm not going to let the moment pass without recognising their talent, and the influence they've had on my view of the world.

And then there are the others – self-serving, self-destructive, tight-arsed cunts who'd happily stab your granny for a bit of cheap publicity.

Like I said earlier, there comes a point when I *will* hit back if I'm pushed far enough – you've been warned.

The B52s

I knew them. Cindy Wilson's voice in songs like 'Girl from Ipanema Goes to Greenland', 'Give Me Back My Man', 'Queen of Los Vegas', 'Moon in Her Mirror', 'Chasing Rainbows', 'She Knows Who', and there's a line in it that says, *'Remember wherever you go, there you are...'* and I very much try and tell people that. They can run and run and run but, often, it's themselves they're running from. 'I'm so unhappy today, I hate London. I've got to go to New York!'

'Hold on, honey, you're the one going to New York. So, wherever you go, there you are.'

Michael Barrymore

My only problem with gay artists like him is, like Barrymore said to somebody, 'I've got his number.' They think they've got me worked out, because Barrymore kept saying to me, 'Drop the act, I can read what you're up to.' And I thought, 'You don't know a damn thing about me, and I know a lot more about you, because you're just desperate for the love of the world.'

It's a need – there's nothing wrong with that. He's more interested in projecting himself at the camera. I saw him do one speech that he went out and rehearsed in the yard for *Big Brother*. There was an argument with George and he cried and he disappeared. Then he came back in and he sat upright in the kitchen, which was raised, so he was centre-stage all the time. It was like a party political broadcast the way he did it, and I went, 'Cut, commercial break,' and left. He totally knew where the camera was – he faced the camera, and he was raised on a stage. Barrymore has got media sickness – that's what it is.

David Bowie

Really, I think my adulation at the time was misdirected, because I realised it was all Angie. It was Angie and, let's face it, what happened to him after she went? *Tin Machine*. I just think David Bowie's Val Doonican with a better suit.

You've only got to listen to *Hunky Dory* and *The Rise and Fall of Ziggy Stardust*. It was really the rise and fall of David Bowie when that divorce came about, because, sometimes, the person who is your muse or is putting the creativity into you, you want them away because you think you can do it yourself, but it's like trying to have a baby without having had a dick up you.

Angie Bowie is creative beyond belief – *Free Spirit, Back Stage Passes*. I've spoken to her. She came out of it with nothing – just the name, and the name doesn't open that many doors for David Bowie these days. So imagine what it's like for her – she'd be way down the food chain.

Boy George

I spoke to George in a very long radio interview – it's all on the website The Right Stuff – all of it. He was such a fan of mine. He had a poster of me in the early 1980s that I didn't know even existed. But there was a phase when BowWowWow were looking for somebody and Malcolm McLaren had gone to Liverpool to try and find me – that's in McLaren's own book. But he couldn't, because by then I'd moved on from Probe Records, and they got Boy George in as Lieutenant Lush to do one number with BowWowWow.

I wasn't aware of him at all until, one day, I went home on the train from Liverpool and people kept saying, 'I saw you on *Top of the Pops*.' I didn't watch *Top of the Pops* then, but they were Number One with 'Do You Really Want to Hurt Me?' And, quite frankly, I did, because, everywhere I went, people were asking me to sign autographs as George. And people who'd seen me on the streets of Liverpool every damn day looking as I did were shouting, 'George! George! George!' and suddenly cab drivers were going, 'I can't believe it! You're tops, aren't you?' I didn't know what they were on about. But I'd not even seem him then – maybe in *The Face* magazine at the squat with a parrot on his head, and Marilyn. That's all.

The bitching between us was created by the press. I

didn't know the game then. Now I know journalists will say, 'So-and-so said such-and-such about you – what are you gonna say?'

'Oh yeah? Fat cunt!' And they'd go right back to him and get another one. I know exactly what they do. We've all had it done to us. The truth is stranger than fiction in this business.

Kate Bush

Oh, she's unbelievable. One of the biggest disappointments to me in my entire life was wanting to record 'Why Should I Love You?' off *Red Shoes* – I thought it was a Prince song. *'The grey of the ghost, the red of the sacred heart, out of all the people in the world, why do I love you?'* Oh, it's so primal... it makes me feel weepy to think about it, it's so great. And that's where a sort of gospel choir take over and they go *'The red of the sacred heart...'* – genius!

Björk

I don't know much about her except she's a bit troubled. But anyone with that amount of talent is going to find communication something of a problem, so it's not surprising she's a bit derailed.

Cabaret

I was too young to get in when it was at the Royal Court in Liverpool. I was just gaga about the idea. I'd seen the photos of Liza and I knew the story – *Goodbye to Berlin* by

Christopher Isherwood – and the character of Sally Bowles was very intriguing. Now it's very much like Truman Capote's Holly Golightly in *Breakfast at Tiffany's*, but more gritty. And after hearing about my mum's past and what Berlin was like and stuff, I somehow got in to see *Cabaret*. I remember I stayed for three shows all day and I kept going back. The choreography, the colours, the night-time world of it, and into the daytime world, this wonderfully vivacious girl was mesmerising.

And the movie floored me – everything about it floored me. The change in the society, the very last shot, where you see the Nazis – there was a very sinister undercurrent running through that film. And the ménage-à-trois situation was very intriguing as well. It was fascinating that she was this seductress with both guys – the rich guy and the poor guy – and she's stuck in the middle with a baby and sells her fur coat and so on… a lot of it sounds like Mum's life, really.

Cher

Somebody who I always really admired and I still do, because of her very being and her beauty. If you look at my 'Rip it Up' video, the Japanese one, Michael Schmidt is a New Yorker who made chain-mail jewellery and accessories and I got friendly with him through a friend. He ended up designing the top of her perfume bottle.

I had met her at the première of *Moonstruck*; I arrived, and everyone thought I was her, and there was a big thing in *Record Mirror* – Cher or Pete Burns? There was a picture of Cher saying something about me – very cartoony, you know.

But I've always admired her. I love her acting, and I love her self-transformation. I do believe that's what she's had to be. I believe her past-life thing – I can see it in her. I loved her book, *The First Time* – I think she tells it like it is. But I bumped into her in Selfridges a few years ago when 'Believe' was out and I just ran up to her and went, 'Oh, God...'

'OK, yeah,' she said, 'I can take that, yeah, yeah, OK.'

'Look, I've got songs I'd love to hear you sing...' I flustered.

'Yeah, yeah, well... OK, I know who you are, OK, bye.'

And she left all her stuff on the counter and she fled the building. She fled! It was as though I was going to mug her.

But she knew who I was. I'd had huge hits in America, and Michael Schmidt, the guy who'd made my stuff, was her stylist. How could she not know who I was? I was number one with 'Come Home with Me, Baby' at the time. I'd just gone up to her to say how great 'Believe' was and thanks for making great records and stuff – and she just fled.

But then I just heard a story from somebody who'd been working with her. He said it's the greatest scene ever when she arrives at an airport – it's straight through on to the tarmac, a big blacked-out limousine, a fleet of support cars... now that's a *real* diva!

Cherry Vanilla

Fabulous. If people don't know about her, they should get her albums *Bad Girl* and *Venus d'Vinyl*. There's nothing to say about Cherry Vanilla other than something's really missing and she deserves to be remembered as a poet, as important as Patti Smith but with less babble. Look up 'I Know How to Hook' and 'Little Red Rooster' – the song about Bowie – and 'Wayne Is Sweet' – about Wayne County – on *Venus d'Vinyl*; or 'Oh So Cool Back in Liverpool' on *Bad Girl*. There's also one called 'Foxy Bitch', which is about God being a woman. Cherry Vanilla was a genius, and one of the few people to whom I'd say, 'Write me a set of lyrics.'

The Cramps

They came over to support The Police at the Liverpool Empire in June 1979. Then they played Eric's, and I hooked up with them. I remember staying in a hotel in Liverpool with them, going to the Everyman Bistro with them and playing The F Club in Leeds and in Manchester with them, and then coming to London to stay at Miles Copeland's house with them.

Bryan, by then, had left The Cramps and he put a band together in LA called the Wild Gypsies and got a deal for it and everything, and I was to be the lead singer. I've got all the letters. I just thought, 'Oh yeah, whatever.' I phoned up Ivy Rorschach, The Cramps' lead guitarist and voodoo expert, and she just thought it was funny and nothing really came of it.

The last I saw of Bryan Gregory, he started to present some kind of horror show on TV. He was great, though. He used to wear those Rolex watches right up his arm and he'd have all these cigarettes on the keys of his guitar and catch them in his mouth. And he had acned skin and that white cascade of hair down his face, but he wore stiletto boots – he was like the ultimate, real macho-looking swaggering star, but with high-heeled shoes. I thought he was great.

Quentin Crisp

Oh, God, oh, God, just for a piece of his mattress! The biggest loss. I knew *The Naked Civil Servant*, but after he died there was a plethora of books. I kept finding more and more information – a New York film called *Resident Alien* and Sting had written that song 'Englishman in New York' and he was in the video and it was like, 'Oh, God!' There's nothing I could say about Quentin Crisp, there isn't a word good enough. It's due to the likes of Quentin Crisp – they were the freedom fighters, they were the people in the trenches and the front line – that made it possible for gay people to date and function.

Divine

The best actress/actor of all time. Divine convinced me and everyone he was a female. You never thought of Divine as a man in drag when you saw him in *Female Trouble* coming down the street in that tigerskin dress and a dose of liquid eyeliner. Never for one minute does it occur to you that's a balding, very gentle and shy man. But, once he put the 'dog' on, he was a persona.

When he recorded with Stock Aitken Waterman, he could not do that vocal without his backless heels on. He kept his tracksuit on or whatever it was he wore, he kept his bald head, but he had to put mules on. The great story was that they made him do a proper vocal and then his manager came and said, 'What the hell's this? Did he have his heels on?' They're thinking, 'What the fuck?' because they'd not seen Divine. They thought it was an old man who'd sung this record! So they dashed to Heathrow, got him back and he goes ,'Oh, OK,' and he got out his Frederick's mules, and went in the vocal booth. He even did that on *Top of the Pops* – they didn't know what they were getting with Divine and he did the whole rehearsal; he had to put the shoes on and instantly he started making magic in those heels!

Homosexuality in Punk

It was quite evident that Sid Vicious was gay; that was a lot to do with his drug problem. Drugs were killing him, because, you know, the punk thing wasn't about homosexuality. It was a very confused free time.

Michael Jackson

I couldn't follow his trial in 2005 because I was in Italy, so we saw the re-enactment on *Court TV*. I'd got the book *Michael Jackson Was My Lover* by Jordi Chandler, years before, and a legal book by somebody who had gone to live in the Dominican Republic because he'd done so much investigation. I found the Chandler book shocking, horrifying, and I saw the Bashir documentary and I just knew they were making a character to suit what they perceived a paedophile looked like. I had also just read extensively about Marie Antoinette and I just thought it really was 'Let's storm the Bastille and pull him from his tower and behead him and root through his belongings.' I thought it was absolutely horrifying but also riveting as well. What did he feel like every day? He could have gone to jail for life. How must he feel now? It must be awful for him. But I think the public know he's innocent – it's just the corporate people who think, 'Right... out!'

The people who think he got away with it – they're just the people with the loudest voices, the wankers. He's non-sexual. The case fell to pieces, and therefore he is innocent. Do the public think that paedophiles have noses like thorns on a rose bud, and wear over-dyed wigs and white foundation? Is that what a paedophile looks like? I beg to differ. They come in many shapes and sizes and many different guises.

Michael Jackson's plastic surgery, it's a work of art. All the photos you've seen of his nose falling off are just Photoshopped. They're not mishaps. That, to me, is some kind of art statement that he's making. The top half of his face is very feminised and the lower half has been over-masculinised – it's like a jigsaw of genders and I wish he could explain that articulately. He's without sex or gender, Michael Jackson, and there are times when I think he is perfectly stunningly beautiful. I think his make-up artist needs shooting, because they just make it all look worse.

I think he just doesn't want anyone close to him. I think he's very self-conscious and trying to guard his image so, consequently, people who are highly inept are keeping him out of reality and I don't think he knows what to do.

I think that the media were putting his plastic surgery and his lifestyle on trial; the kid was nothing to do with it. Suddenly, the public, like fucking harpies, could possibly get a tour around his house and see him without the make-up and the wig. They wanted to storm Neverland – 'Off with his head! Oh, did you abuse the kid? Oh, sorry, we forgot...' Had he been Tupac Shakur and surrounded by women with cannonball boobs in a Jacuzzi and Mai-Tai cocktails with umbrellas in them, they'd have thought it was great. But, because Jackson is surrounded by jack-in-the-boxes and Andy Pandy dolls, people found that really creepy.

Elton John

Fantastic. 'Indian Sunset', that I just love. *Tumbleweed Connection* or one of the earlier ones. And, years later, on *Dances with Wolves*, we get '*This young warrior comes with a bullet hole, I go to search for the other ones, the fathers and sons, but they read some things in the hill, gold without the sign of drums...*' – how fantastic is that? '*As he awoke that evening the smell of wood smoke clinging like a gentle cobweb hanging upon a painted tepee...'* OK, he wouldn't have written that, but listen to the music they build on the orchestration. Sometimes it's like somebody writes it for you, like mediums. In the way I wrote 'Dreamin'' – Debbie Harry just picked up what was going to happen in my life.

Elton came and introduced himself to us at the Montreux Festival but I was just too shy to speak to him. I've met him since and he's adorable. He really took care of me at a David LaChapelle exhibition when the paparazzi went crazy and I didn't know why.

John Lydon

Fabulous. Just generally... what was that great record, *Burn Hollywood Burn*? I didn't see him in the *I'm a Celebrity...* jungle thing, but his principles, his intellect, his gentleness all shine through. An angel. He's a gentle soul.

LaBelle

Yeah, I love LaBelle. Nona Hendryx – fantastic, she was one of LaBelle. The glam-rock thing, outer space, very like Ziggy, although I liked Jobriath, another of the glam-rock school at the time, better than David Bowie. Jobriath was much more interesting than David Bowie to me, because he was out of space with the silver helmet and that was like *Barbarella*. I remember him on *The Old Grey Whistle Test* when he took the silver helmet off and then underneath was this incredibly painted face. Lindsay Kemp was innovating with style and movement at the time, and I remember a play he did called *Flowers* with a guy in a sailor's uniform with blue eye-shadow and a short-back-and-sides – the beauty of those things. I so much wanted to get to London and be among those 1970s movers and shakers, like Lindsay Kemp, Duggie Fields, Andrew Logan, Luciana Martinez and Zandra Rhodes.

Marilyn Manson

Silly cunt. Satanism? Oh, come on... I read his biography and I thought, 'What a pile of crap!' Antone LeVay and the church of Satan? It's like whatever Marc Almond perpetuated in the early days, all those dark sleeves – Marilyn Manson bought it from the wholesaler's and is trying to run with it. I think it's a tragedy – he looks like a hard-boiled egg with make-up on. Also, his biggest hits are cover versions, so what does that say? I have absolutely no time, no time at all, in my breathing schedule for Marilyn Manson. Alice Cooper did it years ago and did it better.

Mel & Kim

Big loss. Oh, they were just so lovely, lots of laughter – you can hear them laughing on the record. Stock Aitken Waterman wrote 'Respectable' for me, but I couldn't do it, but then they came in and it was meant to be. It was serendipity, wasn't it? When I heard the Mel & Kim album, there was a song called 'Sisters' and the voices are just fabulous. Those cheeky little dances they did. Makes me happy that Mel & Kim album, inspired me again. They make you want to curl your hair and go out.

George Michael

Fabulous. That voice, the songwriting ability, the way he's trying to tell people even in that song, 'You're Amazing', the liner notes of that album about him and his lover… He needs something, George Michael – one's not enough – he needs the validation, maybe, of those sexual dalliances, and his boyfriend obviously understands that. Because some people need more than one person can give and, just because it's a need, doesn't mean that it's wrong. Some people need insulin – it doesn't mean that there's anything wrong with them. So he needs more than his boyfriend can give and his lover obviously loves him, so you get *'But I love you, you love me, you get that.'* I think it's cool.

I couldn't do that in a relationship. I'm not benevolent enough to do that – I'm a one-man man. I just couldn't do it. I'd feel… I have clothes, and if someone wears my sweater, which they can, they can have it. I don't want it back – I don't want to lend things. If someone wants something, don't steal it – ask and I'll give it you. I'm like that with the idea of a relationship. It's like, 'Don't push me off the throne – just ask me and I'll move along. You're welcome to it.'

Kylie Minogue

I feel very sorry for her and her fight against breast cancer. I don't know her at all, but I'm not impressed by her music. It's sad that Kylie's become such a gay icon, because ultimately the gay iconography of women is usually because they're so tragic – Judy and Marilyn, that's gay iconography. But now, most of gay culture tends to think that gay culture started with Kylie's arse and it's not so, because the gay population is very uneducated as to where they came from and why they're there. One day, Judy Garland will be forgotten and *'the man that got away'*. They'd rather listen to 'Can't Get You Out of My Head', or Dannii Minogue. I'd rather listen to Danny La Rue.

Marilyn Monroe

The Misfits, that's the only movie I liked. It was almost like she was under water, and as a photographic object, the ones where she was coming to pieces; she had a frailty that was very beautiful. But not that baby voice and 'Happy Birthday, Mr President' – I found that really irritating because I've heard all of her tapes doing interviews with the psychoanalyst Dr Ralph Greenson.

I stayed at Marilyn Monroe's house in LA – I rented 12305 Cliff Helena Drive and it's a very modest house, not where you'd expect a movie star to live. It was like a bungalow, very isolated, a very lonely spot for a murder. And I do believe she was murdered, because of all the latest evidence that I've seen and the reports.

First of all, she didn't die in the bedroom, she died in the guesthouse. The drugs were administered with an enema. It was obviously a murder, whether it was the CIA or Castro's people or Kennedy's.

But she was a woman ahead of her time. In this day and age, she would have been Monica Lewinsky. It was a very sinister place to stay, there was death all round that place.

There is a death tour of Hollywood, but we went independently in a car because I wanted to see things for myself. I also went to where Sharon Tate, the actress and wife of Roman Polanski, was murdered. They've changed the number on Shallow Drive now and it's at the top of a winding hill. There's a recording studios there now, and bands stay there.

Hollywood itself is incredibly morbid. It has desperate people at both ends of the scale. There's a desperation in Hollywood that's bigger than the Earth. It's tawdry, it's desperate. Every waiter will do anything. As soon as you're halfway from the airport heading into the low hills of Hollywood, you can sense the desperation. It's fascinating – it's like a movie you know. I don't like to be there very long, though.

Ozzy Osbourne

I think he's fabulous. I only saw a few episodes of his show *The Osbournes*, but I think he's fab. I like the family unit. I don't think it's dysfunctional – I think it's a real family. They swear, they have arguments, the kids go out on the razz, they have drug problems, they're going to rehab, there's the mother who just appears to me like the most fabulous mother there could possibly be – and manager. I'd love to be managed by Sharon Osbourne, but you wouldn't get the same treatment unless you were from her womb. I love her.

Pet Shop Boys

Fantastic – what can I say? Marlene Dietrich, Pet Shop Boys – the understatement of song. For someone to sing a gay anthem like 'Go West' and somehow emote the sadness of the loss of that gay freedom in the San Francisco days, which even I was reading about pre-Sylvester, knowing what was going on in San Francisco and thinking that must be the place to go. They capture that in 'Go West' – *'Life is peaceful there...'* – it's a bygone time. That time went – it's over and it'll never be like that again. Now it's a war.

Elvis Presley

I loved that shop in London, Elvisly Yours, and I loved his eye-shadow and his photos. I thought he was one of the most beautiful men that ever lived, and a couple of his songs were great, but I wasn't an Elvis fan. I just had a lot of Elvis bits and pieces.

I went to Graceland during the 1980s specifically to buy the slippers with the revolving head that sang *Love Me Tender*, and some Elvis Presley toilet paper that had a song title on every sheet. I loved Graceland – it was like a council house with a big façade. It's hilarious. And I loved Priscilla's look when she married him. Sonny & Cher and Elvis and Priscilla looked so alike, didn't they? I think he wore more make-up than she did really, but I just love that look.

Queen and Freddie Mercury

I appreciate everything that they did, and what a vocal talent Freddie had. My least favourite one's 'Bohemian Rhapsody', but everything else, like 'Killer Queen', is fab. And that gay clone look – that's sort of double cross-dressing, isn't it? It's like a lot of women now look like drag queens and drag queens look like a lot of women that have gone before. So it's a case of double cross-dressing. A woman dressing as a man dressing as a woman.

The Queen and the Royal Family

I mean, what a shitty job, but someone's got to do it. It's very important we have that – look at the industry it brings to and from England. Without them, we'd be a country on our arse. Yeah, the Queen's fabulous. And look now how the monarchy has opened up – Vivienne Westwood's been made a Dame!

Diana Ross

She's a great deliverer of songs. I've been listening to 'Ain't No Mountain High Enough' and I play that bit again and again where she squeals – just those little bits that she does, she doesn't need to do much. On the last record she did, 'I'm Not Over You Yet', she goes *'Baby...'* – the classic Diana Ross thing – and, oh, genius! Scrap the ballads and get a decent wig.

Dennis Rodman

We used to call Dennis Rodman 'Fluffy', because he was so gentle. Dennis Rodman would kiss a bird with a broken wing. He stole my cigarettes for me, he folded my clothes. If I had a pain in my back, he'd massage it. I was like his jail bitch, except I didn't have to do anything for it. And he bought me a huge black rubber sheet for my bed. But why black? I only like them in gold. He was a tiny little angel trapped in a great big bull's body.

Roxy Music

I love Bryan Ferry's *As Time Goes By* album. Bryan Ferry – 'Slave to Love' – a great deliverer of a song. Brian Eno goes to my gym, I see him all the time. Wasn't it great when Roxy Music did 'Virginia Plain'? You couldn't top it. Eno's jacket with the plumes. I loved the cover artwork; I loved Amanda as black on black with the jaguar and the chauffeur, the night-time look, it was always very night-time. Songs like 'Sentimental Fool' and 'Love Is the Drug' – yeah, must get those again.

RuPaul

Got a phone call from him the other night. He gave me a big break in America and put me on *The RuPaul Show* a while ago. He's just wonderful, RuPaul. A 7-foot-tall basketball-playing, black motherfucker – as if you're ever going to get in the charts as a 7-foot drag queen! But he got to the top, and won acceptance in middle America. Why? Because he did it so damn well. If you do something that well, people can't help but say, 'You know what, that's genius.'

So I love RuPaul. Even without his make-up he's a wonderful-looking man. But that's drag, too – he's in preppy drag. Because RuPaul's a spirit and a soul – that's why he can be both. He's male and female, so he can be both – he's just a spirit, so both sides are lovely.

Paul Rutherford

An old acquaintance and friend. We sort of grew up together but not as much as people would say. He's had an incredible amount of hard knocks in his life and he continues to sail and good things come to Paul, but he has a lot of tragedy around him. He's a good spirit, Paul. He lives in New Zealand now.

He doesn't do heavy – he's had too much heavy in his life, so he won't go there. You can't discuss serious subjects with Paul because none of your problems is as big as what he's been through and overcome. So, if you go to Paul, you're depressed, you've got a headache, you've got no money, he's like, 'Oh fuck it,' but it just doesn't touch him.

Johnny Thunders

He wanted to sleep with me. I met Johnny – the front man for the New York Dolls – through Lee Black Childers and they had a flat in Soho and it was just obvious. He got undressed and he was naked but he couldn't get an erection, and he was trying to kiss me. And he did kiss me, and I kissed him right back as well, but then he crashed out unconscious. I actually thought he was really cute because he just went – crash!

We went to a few places on Oxford Street in the early hours of the morning – this was the 1970s – and I'd just think, 'Oh, he must be so tired because he's fallen asleep face down in his chicken and sweetcorn soup in a Chinese restaurant.' There were other people there and I was saying, 'Oh, God, he's so tired. Shouldn't we get him back to the flat?' I had no idea!

Transvision Vamp

Zeus B Held did them as well. How great were Transvision Vamp? They had a history. Transvision Vamp were as important as Blondie. That girl – Wendy James – great pop star she was. Said all the wrong things, wore all the wrong clothes, wore far too much make-up, smoked too much – that was a pop star! And yet who mentions Transvision Vamp now, ever? And what great records! 'Tell That Girl To Shut Up'... And what's more, she hated my guts. She judged one of my videos on TV and said, 'Just a stupid poofy boy with poofy hairdo.' I just loved her! Fabulous!

Rufus Wainwright

Adore him. I saw him on *Jools Holland* recently, and I've been sent some of his lyrics but he doesn't know who the hell I am, apparently.

But I prefer Janis Ian – American singer, songwriter, poet... I've just bought all the back catalogue. That song '17', and 'Star', she's a real talent.

John Waters

The extraordinary film-maker from Baltimore – genius. If you think of anywhere in the world that's repressed and grey, there are often great people to be found from there because they've gone, 'Oh, gotta get out of here!' They get a sense of humour at other people's expense, which is fundamentally the ingredient of humour.

People can call me a bitch or a wise-crack, but the very nature of humour is always at someone else's expense, like the Englishman, the Irishman and the Scotsman. Stand-up comedians pick on one at the table and everyone laughs at them. Laughter is often induced by a kind of embarrassment, it's uncomfortable. So you burst out laughing because you're uncomfortable. Funny, to me, is when something unusual happens, and humour is not unusual.

John Waters has got his own brand of humour. He did a book called *Crackpot*, which I read when I was depressed and I just couldn't stop laughing at the whole story of the Howard Hughes thing, wearing tissue boxes on his feet, or Edith Massey – who was the egg lady in *Pink Flamingos* and *Female Trouble* – it's just genius.

Pete Waterman

His total childlike optimism is what makes him see no reason why he can't make something happen. He doesn't see the rules.

He'd just burst through the studio door, listen for ten seconds and say, 'It needs more blue in it.' Then he'd disappear. Then he'd go, 'Now it needs more stars.' And then he'd disappear again and come back two days later and go, 'Where's the glitter?' He's an explosion of creativity. I'd love to work with him again. I love the man. I can't bear to be in the same room as him, but the same building is tolerable!

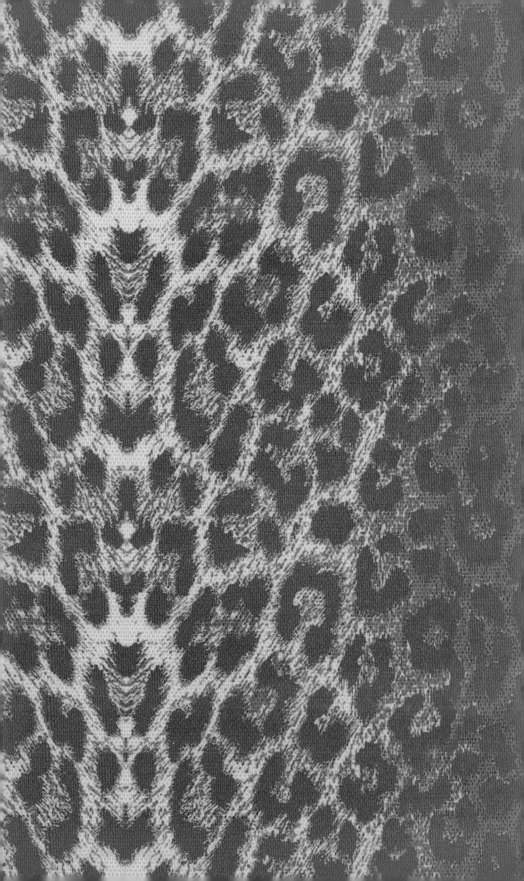